THE CHEESE LIFE

An Hachette UK Company
www.hachette.co.uk

First published in Great Britain in 2023 by Kyle Books, an imprint of Octopus Publishing
Group Limited, Carmelite House, 50 Victoria Embankment, London, EC4Y 0DZ

ISBN: 978 1 80419 154 5

Distributed in the US by Hachette Book Group,
1290 Avenue of the Americas, 4th and 5th Floors, New York, NY 10104
Distributed in Canada by Canadian Manda Group,
664 Annette St., Toronto, Ontario, Canada M6S 2C8

Publishing Director: Judith Hannam
Publisher: Joanna Copestick
Editor: Isabel Jessop
Design: Praline (Michael Curia and David Tanguy)
Photographer: Lizzie Mayson
Food Stylist: Rosie Reynolds
Prop Stylist: Louie Waller
Production: Emily Noto

A Cataloguing in Publication record for this title is available from the British Library.

Printed and bound in China.

10 9 8 7 6 5 4 3 2 1

Additional image permissions: 6 top left, © Mathew Carver, 2023; 6 top centre, © Simon
Mills, 2023; 6 top right, © Nic Crilly-Hargrave, 2023; 6 centre right, © Mathew Carver,
2023; 6 bottom left, Nic Crilly-Hargrave, 2023; 6 bottom right, © Mathew Carver, 2023;
10 top left, © Mathew Carver, 2023; 10 top centre, © Mathew Carver, 2023; 10 top right,
© Mathew Carver, 2023; 10 centre far left (barge), © Brotherton Lock, 2023; 10 centre left
(chefs), © Nic Crilly-Hargrave, 2023; 10 centre right, © Mathew Carver, 2023; 10 bottom
left, © Mathew Carver, 2023; 10 bottom centre, © Mathew Carver, 2023; 10 bottom right,
© J Howard, 2023; 14, photo by Robbe Musschoot; 17, © Simon Mills, 2023 (what makes
good cheese); 20, © Nic Crilly-Hargrave, 2023 (how to buy cheese); 40, © Simon Mills,
2023; 51, © Nic Crilly-Hargrave, 2023 (cheddar being opened); 59, © Simon Mills, 2023
(affinage); 78, © Simon Mills, 2023 (blue cheese); 92, © Paxton & Whitfield, 2023;
93, © Harry Darby, 2023; 128, photo by Matt Horwood, © The Guild of Fine Food, 2023;
144, photo by André Pattenden © Trethowan's Dairy, 2023 (crumbly); 155, © The Cheese Bar,
2023 (how to eat cheese); 182, all photos © Isabelle Plasschaert, 2023 (pairing + pouring)

Mathew Carver and Patrick McGuigan

THE CHEESE LIFE

Recipes, Cheeseboards and Pairings

Grill

24

Melt

60

Bake

94

GRATE

130

SLICE

158

LIVING THE CHEESE LIFE

There's something in the air in British cheese shops, and it's not just the tempting aroma of Cheddar and Stilton. Breathe in deeply and you will also pick up notes of love, obsession and even a subtle hint of revolution.

That's because there's been a remarkable renaissance in the quality and range of cheeses being made in this country, driven by a new generation of farmers, cheesemakers, cheesemongers and chefs, who are fully committed to leading their best cheese lives.

This book is a celebration of this turnaround, packed with stories about the people and cheeses that have helped put British cheese back on the map, plus killer recipes from The Cheese Truck and The Cheese Bar restaurants (more on them later).

To understand exactly why and how this happened requires a quick history lesson. At the start of the twentieth century, there were thousands of small, farm-based cheesemakers in Britain. But two world wars, government supports for milk and the rise of large creameries meant that by the 1960s there were just a few dozen traditional cheesemakers left.

But the beginnings of a fight-back came in the 1980s when a handful of new cheesemakers set up as part of a British "back-to-the-land", smallholder movement. Their numbers swelled in the 1990s as chefs became celebrities and the British restaurant scene took off, a trend that continued into the 2000s with farmers' markets and a surge in interest in local food. The Cheese Truck and the Cheese Bar restaurants are part of the story too, bringing good British cheese to festival goers at Glastonbury and diners in central London.

Today the UK has more than 200 small cheesemakers, many of whom are young and enthusiastic, and are winning awards on the international stage. There are also hundreds of delis, farm shops, cheesemongers and cheese-obsessed restaurants for them to sell to. British cheese is even being exported to France.

The people that work in these businesses have created their own unique cheese culture and community. Cheese is not just a job. It's a way of life for many and they have the tattoos to prove it, with arms inked with artwork depicting cows, cheese knives and cartoon wedges.

Most people don't set out to work in cheese. They find themselves falling into it as a career, so everyone has a story to tell. There are plenty of actors, musicians, artists and writers who end up becoming cheesemongers and makers, but we also know accountants, lawyers, chefs and scaffolders who have heard the cheese calling.

This culture is not just confined to the UK. Similar scenes have sprung up in the US, Japan and Australia, which have undergone their own cheese revolutions, while a new wave of young *fromagers* are breaking traditions in France and Spain.

Despite the success story, British artisan cheese remains a fledgling industry. It's a small world where everyone seems to know everyone. Perhaps that is why it is so unusually open and friendly, with close links between the farms, cheesemakers, cheesemongers and chefs.

What unites everyone living the cheese life around the world is a mad passion for the food itself. There's something about the way cheese is rooted in the land and history that seems to capture the imagination. That sense of place, seasonality, craft skills, mysterious microbes and the sheer deliciousness of cheese make it irresistible for anyone interested in food.

That's true as much for the farmers who spend their days in the fields and milking parlours as it is for the cheesemakers, who bend their backs in warm dairies, transforming milk into rounds and truckles. And it's especially true for the cheesemongers, chefs and waiters who unwrap, slice and serve cheese every day, providing the cities and towns with a direct link back to the fields and farms where the cheese was made.

There's more than one type of cheese life.

Mathew

People have romantic visions of how journeys like mine start out. "He must REALLY love cheese," they say, some deep-rooted passion that drives him on. The truth is far less glamorous and much more serendipitous than you'd believe.

My story starts with a desire to escape the hum-drum of office life and spend my days at music festivals. I also had to find a use for a 1970s ice-cream van I was gifted. Dishing out grilled cheese sandwiches to intoxicated revellers at Glastonbury seemed like the natural solution.

My first ever grilled cheese sandwich was served on 6 February 2014. Me and my friend Alex Lambert bought some British artisan cheese, namely Keen's Cheddar, Ogleshield and Cropwell Bishop Stilton, pitched a stall at Maltby Street Market, London, and flogged about 20 sandwiches to predominately supportive friends. Alex is the first of many people who shaped our story; we wouldn't be where we are today without them.

The more I learned about British cheese, the more fascinated I became. Firstly, because it tasted incredible! But, also, because the stories, the people and the creativity that come when passion is put before profit really inspired me.

Back then, most of my friends could name more European cheeses than they could British. That just didn't seem right. I wanted to serve incredible British cheeses in a way that would engage a new audience, bringing fun and youthful energy, and encouraging people to discover the exceptional cheesemakers on their doorstep.

So that summer we took our converted ice-cream van (painted yellow and christened Archie) to Glastonbury and sold 4,000 grilled cheese sandwiches over the weekend, all filled with the best British cheese we could find.

I suppose that's when I really started to live the cheese life.

To save some time and vital pages, I thought it would be easier to summarize our glory years in a timeline:

6 February 2014
The Cheese Truck is born, sans truck! We take a stall on Maltby Street Market and sell our first grilled cheese sandwiches.

25 June 2014
The Cheese Truck is actually born. Our first event in the Truck is Glastonbury Festival.

3 March 2017
We open The Cheese Bar in London's famous Camden Market.

8 September 2019
Pick & Cheese, the world's first cheese conveyor belt restaurant, opens in Covent Garden, London.

22 October 2020
Funk, our cheese and bottle shop, opens on Columbia Road in East London.

21 May 2021
The Cheese Barge, our 96-foot floating restaurant devoted to British Cheese, opens outside Paddington Station, London.

So, that's two cheese trucks, three cheese restaurants, one cheese shop and countless tonnes of artisan British cheese in less than 10 years.

Today, we serve thousands of customers a week in our restaurants and shop. And we live by the motto "Eat More British Cheese". I like to think we've become an important part of the new wave of cheesemongers, makers and retailers pushing the industry forward in Britain. It's never been a more exciting time to embrace good cheese!

Real cheese tastes better, does better and melts better. But it shouldn't be intimidating or complicated. So join me and my good friend Patrick as we take you on a journey into cheese and demystify what can at first seem complex and confusing. We're serious about great produce, but not so serious that we forget to enjoy ourselves. Cheese is fun, food should be fun, and life should be fun! Otherwise why bother....

Hang on, who's Patrick? Well, I'll let him introduce himself, but a quick story about the first time I spoke to him. It was a Monday morning, 28 June 2015. I'd just woken up in a sweltering tent at Glastonbury after our second year at the festival. We'd sold somewhere in the region of 12,000 grilled cheese sandwiches, I'd had precisely nine hours of sleep in five days and I smelled quite strongly of cheese.

Who do you want to be on the phone call that wakes you up? I'll tell you who you don't want it to be... a journalist writing an article for the *Telegraph* hoping for an interview with you! Thanks Patrick. Luckily, I held it together, managed to say a few vaguely coherent things and the friendship with Patrick was born. He's been one of our biggest supporters and a great source of cheese knowledge to us ever since.

Hopefully you'll come away from our book with an understanding of what makes real cheese important. How to buy, cook, talk and share it with confidence and gusto. You'll also hopefully come away with the same admiration and love for good cheese that I have.

Patrick

It's funny, I can also clearly remember the day I called Mathew for that article. It was for a piece on how British cheese was having a moment, thanks to a new generation of dynamic young cheesemakers and retailers (and street food traders) who were breathing new life into an industry that had long struggled. It ran with the headline, "The only whey is British: the great cheese revolution," which summed up the mood quite nicely.

The thing that first struck me when chatting to Mathew was not that he was hungover in a tent – my investigative journalism skills somehow missed that – but that he had sold over a tonne of artisan British cheese in just one weekend at Glastonbury. That's a lot of grilled cheese sandwiches (Mathew made it clear several times that I must not call them toasties in the article).

Up until this point, the British cheese renaissance had been taking place rather quietly in specialist cheese shops, farmers' markets and high-end restaurants, where older, affluent customers were the norm. But here was someone serving some of the best cheese in the land to young festival goers, and they were clearly absolutely loving it.

It turned out Mathew was only just getting started. I've written numerous articles since then about how he has built his cheese empire, flying the flag for artisan British cheese with passion, creativity and a commitment to showcasing small family producers. Mind you, if you can't get a story out of the launch of a cheese conveyor belt restaurant, then you might as well give up being a journalist.

We ended up working together to put on three cheese festivals called The London Cheese Project with our cheesemaker pal Kristen Schnepp, one in Camden and two in Hackney. Thousands of people, most of them in their 20s and 30s, came to buy direct from cheesemakers, attend talks and tastings, and generally stuff themselves silly with melted cheese, while necking craft beer to live music.

We wanted to capture that fun and vibrancy in this book, telling some of the stories behind the cheeses we love and the people that make them.

I've spent the past 15 years visiting and interviewing many of them in what has turned into my own unusual little cheese life, full of weird and wonderful moments. I've trekked in the Picos de Europa mountains in Spain in search of caves filled with Cabrales blue cheese, made Cheddar in Cheddar Gorge and dined in hipster cheese bars in New York.

Wherever I've gone, I've been struck by the kindness and openness of people working in cheese. They want to tell me about their history, their land and their animals. They're always happy to show me how they make and mature their cheeses. And they've welcomed me into their shops and restaurants with great warmth, giving me tastes of their favourite wedges and the wines they go best with.

We want to bring all these different lives and stories together in one place, so as you read the book, you'll hear two different voices. Mathew has collated the recipes, which come from years spent building his cheese truck and restaurant empire. I have written the sections explaining the how, why, who and where of good cheese, taking you behind the scenes of the wonderful world in which we are both so immersed.

In other words, we want to dig beneath the rind and give you the knowledge and confidence to buy and eat great cheese.

Welcome to the cheese life!

WHAT MAKES GOOD CHEESE?

Life is too short for boring cheese. Whether you're making a grilled cheese sandwich or a spectacular cheeseboard, our advice is to buy the best cheese you can. It might cost more, but it will taste better and last longer in the memory.

But what exactly is the best cheese?

Well, it's complicated. Ask that question to a room full of cheesemongers and you will receive twice as many opinions as there are people in aprons. But cheesemongers are an affable bunch and they usually agree on a few fundamentals.

Cheeses made by hand on a small scale are more interesting than those made by machines in big creameries. Sometimes called "farmhouse" or "artisan" cheeses, they are often made with milk from a single herd or flock and have complex and subtle flavours that reflect the seasons and the craft of the cheesemaker.

Raw milk can also be a good sign. It suggests higher welfare standards on the farm and an interest in traditional cheesemaking in the dairy. Pasteurization involves heating milk to kill off any harmful bacteria. This is done as a food safety precaution. In the US, the Food and Drug Administration requires that raw milk cheeses must be aged for at least 60 days, which rules out lots of young, soft raw milk cheeses. But this is not a requirement everywhere. Many cheesemakers, who are confident their milk is clean and safe, don't pasteurize, thereby retaining the good natural bacteria in the raw milk. These unique microbes, which are specific to the land, animals, farm and dairy, can create complex flavours that make a cheese sing.

While these are all good rules of thumb, there are always exceptions. We've tasted terrible cheeses from small farms using unpasteurized milk. Similarly, there are some great cheeses from large dairies.

It's worth digging a bit deeper.

The farm

There's an argument cheese is made in the field, not the dairy. "You can't make good cheese with bad milk," is a phrase cheesemakers often say.

Most milk in the UK comes from black and white cows (Holstein–Friesians), which have been bred to produce huge volumes of milk. As a nation of tea and cereal lovers, the UK has an insatiable demand for liquid milk, and the dairy industry has responded by expanding the size of herds, farming more intensively and breeding cows that can produce Herculean amounts of milk. Some cows rarely see the light of day because they are kept in sheds and fed silage (pickled grass and other crops), cereals and protein.

Smaller farms focused on cheesemaking tend not to push their animals so hard. They are more likely to graze their animals for longer and many are also reintroducing native and traditional breeds that are hardier and produce richer milk. If you see a cheese made with milk from Montbéliarde, Guernsey, Jersey, Shorthorn or Ayrshire cows, then it's definitely worth further investigation. The same goes for sheep breeds, such as Lacaune and Lleyn, and goats, such as Anglo–Nubian or Golden Guernsey.

Diet also makes a difference to the flavour of cheese. Cows that are free to graze, especially if the pasture contains diverse grasses, herbs and flowers, produce better milk for cheese.

Sensory trials in Ireland found that Cheddar made with milk from free-grazing cows tasted better than those made with milk from indoor, ration-fed animals. The cheeses were softer and more yellow and had a higher concentration of "good" fats, including conjugated linoleic acid. Similar research into the French cheese Cantal showed that cheeses from pasture-fed cows tasted creamier and had more intense flavours.

There's been a move among British farm-based cheesemakers to improve pastures in recent years as part of the regenerative agriculture movement, which has seen them sowing a much wider range of plants in their fields. Grasses, herbs and legumes with wonderful names such as timothy, yarrow, sheep's parsley and bird's-foot trefoil. Known as herbal leys, they help capture carbon and fix nitrogen in the soil, meaning less need for artificial fertilizers, and improved biodiversity and soil health. They also provide a more varied diet for the grazing animals, leading to better milk and more delicious cheeses.

The idea is that like terroir in wine, cheeses made on a farm with animals grazing diverse pastures have unique personalities and a sense of place.

The dairy

Not surprisingly, the cheesemaker has a big say in how the final cheese turns out. Milk changes dramatically depending on the season, the animal's diet, its lactation cycle and even the weather.

Some large creameries with automated equipment will standardize their milk, removing or adding fat and protein, so that the equipment runs smoothly and the cheese remains consistent. But smaller dairies roll with the seasonal differences in the milk. Their cheeses will taste different depending on the time of year, but that's what makes it delicious and interesting.

Then there's the process itself. While larger creameries work at huge scale, using automated machinery overseen by engineers, traditional cheesemakers work with open vats, using a mix of science, intuition and experience. Rather than follow a recipe, the best cheesemakers adjust and adapt what they do, guided by how the milk and curd looks, feels, smells and tastes.

This instinctive knowledge, accumulated over generations, is also at play in the maturing room. How cheeses are looked after as they age can have a huge impact on their final flavour and texture in a way that simply doesn't apply to cheeses that are vacuum packed in plastic (see pages 58–59).

One last, important point. What constitutes "good cheese" is not just about flavour and texture. While cheeses made by hand on farms are invariably more delicious than those made in big factories, their creation also keeps alive skills and traditions that stretch back generations. They reflect the climate, geography, economy and history of the place where they are made in a way that factory cheeses rarely do. They also provide employment and investment in local areas.

They are certainly not boring.

DAIRY MAGIC: HOW CHEESE IS MADE

Making cheese is like alchemy. With a bit of magic, a liquid is transformed into a solid. Milk becomes curd.

There are lots of books and courses on how this happens (it's science not sorcery), but a good way to understand it is by looking at the four main ingredients involved: milk, starter cultures, rennet and salt.

Milk

You can make cheese from almost any type of milk. Horse, camel, reindeer and donkey cheeses are popular in some parts of the world, but the big four are cow, sheep, goat and buffalo.

Milk is nutritious stuff, rich in protein and fat, which are the building blocks of cheese. When milk curdles, the previously soluble proteins join together to form a wobbly curd, trapping fat and moisture in the process.

Starter cultures

Cheese is a fermented food, so to get the process going, helpful bacteria, known as starter cultures, are added to the milk. These micro-organisms convert the natural sugars (lactose) in milk into lactic acid.

If you've ever squeezed lemon juice into milk, you'll know that acidity will cause it to split and curdle. The same thing can happen with starter cultures. Leave them long enough in the milk and they produce so much lactic acid that the proteins clump together to create a delicate blancmange-like curd. A lot of goats' cheeses are made this way and are sometimes referred to as "lactic cheeses".

Starter cultures also play other crucial roles in cheese, helping to make it a safe food (potentially harmful bacteria struggle to survive in acidic environments) and creating different flavours in the final cheese.

Rennet

To help the curdling process (known as coagulation), rennet is also often used. This is an enzyme, extracted from the fourth stomach of a calf, kid or lamb, which changes the proteins in the milk so they stick together to form a more solid curd than through acidity alone. There are also vegetarian rennets, which have been developed in laboratories, and plant-based alternatives, such as cardoon thistles, which do a similar job.

Once you've got your curd, you can do all sorts of different things with it depending on what style of cheese you want to make, from simply ladling it into moulds to make soft cheese, to cutting, heating, piling and pressing the curd to reduce the amount of moisture (whey) and make harder cheeses for longer ageing.

Salt

The final ingredient is salt, normally added at the end of the process to help preservation and to flavour. This can be done by sprinkling salt on the curds before they are moulded into shape. Alternatively, the cheese is formed and floated in a brine bath. For small soft cheeses the cheesemaker will just rub dry salt on the outside.

Hey presto, you have cheese.

HOW TO BUY CHEESE

If you're going to take one thing away from this book, then we hope it's this piece of advice: buy your cheese from a cheesemonger.

The people that work behind cheese counters in specialist shops are literally living the cheese life. Their job is to find the best cheeses, keep them in the best conditions and tell anyone who will listen why they are so good. They'll also let you taste before you buy and are full of excellent advice about how to cook with cheese and what to drink with it.

So if you have a deli, farm shop, food hall or even better a dedicated cheese shop near you, get in there and get chatting to the cheesemonger. And if you don't have one near you, there's always online – they all deliver. (See pages 200–201 for a list of good shops in the UK and other parts of the world.)

Cheesemonger chat

A few tips when you are in a cheese shop. Don't be shy. Talk to the cheesemonger. Tell them what you like and don't like, what you want the cheese for and how much you want to spend. They don't want to judge you. They want to talk to you about cheese and help you find your perfect wedge.

Cheeses that are freshly cut from a larger wheel will be in better condition than pre-wrapped pieces. And don't buy too much in one go. It's better to buy what you need, so that it's in good condition when you taste it, rather than huge pieces that will sit in your refrigerator and become dry and cracked. Little and often is the rule.

When it comes to oozy woozy cheeses, such as Brie, washed rinders and blues, it's also a good idea to tell the cheesemonger when you're going to be eating it. If you're buying Brie on a Monday, but not going to eat it until Saturday, the cheesemonger should hopefully sell you a cheese that is a little under ripe, but will be gloriously gooey by the weekend.

Supermarket strategies

That's not to say it's impossible to buy good cheese in a supermarket. It just needs a bit of a know-how.

First of all, pick your retailer. In the UK, Waitrose, M&S and Booths are the best supermarkets for cheese. In the US, Whole Foods Market and Kroger (which has Murray's Cheese counters) are the pick of the bunch. In Europe, try Eataly (Italy), Biocoop (France), El Corte Inglés (Spain) and Biomarkt (Germany). In Australia, there are a growing number of upmarket Cole's and Woolworth's stores.

When you get there, head to the counter if they have one, and chat to the cheesemonger. If there isn't one and you find yourself in the pre-wrapped cheese aisle, then go for retailers' premium own brands. They will have been aged for longer and been specially selected by graders (cheese tasters) to have richer, stronger and more balanced flavours. They will cost more, but you get what you pay for.

Avoid pre-sliced and pre-grated cheeses, which can be dry and plastic-tasting, but soft cheeses in wooden and card boxes can be good, such as Camembert and Epoisses. The packaging helps protect the cheese and acts almost like a little cave.

Read the labels closely. Cheeses that are made with raw or organic milk, or give specific information about the farm or breed of animal, could be interesting. But be careful of marketing smoke and mirrors. Just because the word "farm" appears in the brand name, doesn't actually mean it's made on a farm.

Cheeses that are protected under Geographical Indication laws are also worth looking out for. They are governed by strict rules, designed to protect traditional practices and recipes, such as the use of raw milk from particular breeds and traditional rennet. Comté, Roquefort, Parmigiano Reggiano, Stilton, feta and Mozzarella di Bufala Campana are just some of those covered by the schemes. The most common logos to look for are "Protected Designation of Origin" (PDO) or "Protected Geographical Indication" (PGI), which are regulated by the EU.

There are equivalent national protections, which mean the same thing, such as Designated Origin and Geographic Origin in the UK, Appellation d'Origine Protégée (AOP) in France and Switzerland and Denominazione d'Origine Protetta (DOP) in Italy.

How to keep cheese

The cool temperature, high humidity and gentle airflow of caves and cellars have long made them the perfect places for maturing cheese.

Unfortunately, not many houses or apartments are equipped with either, but you can use the salad drawer in your refrigerator as a kind of mini cave for cheese (who needs salad anyway?). It will protect cheese from the worst of the air flow that is blown around domestic refrigerators.

Waxed paper is king when it comes to wrapping. It's favoured by cheesemongers because it protects cheese from drying out, while also allowing it to breath. If you buy your cheese from a cheese shop, try not to rip the paper as you open it so you can use it to re-wrap. But don't swap wrappers between cheeses because moulds and aromas will jump from one to another. Friendly

mongers might even give you a few sheets to take home with you, if you ask nicely. It's really important to wrap your cheese tightly with no exposed areas, so it doesn't dry out (see pages 194–195 for wrapping techniques).

Cling film (plastic wrap) works pretty well on hard cheese, but soft and sticky cheeses can get sweaty and their delicate rinds can suffocate under plastic. Reusable beeswax cloth wraps are better for the environment, but not always easy to wrap snugly around the cheese. For super pungent cheeses that fill the refrigerator with their funky fragrance, airtight containers are a wise move. Just remember to take the lid off every day or two to let the cheese breathe.

Finally, if some of your cheese starts to grow moulds, then don't worry too much. Just scrape or slice off the offending areas and re-wrap nice and tight.

Cheese is a living food that needs a bit of looking after.

Cheese styles: The Magnificent Seven

Fresh
One step away from milk, these young, soft and mild cheeses are made to be eaten within hours or days of being created. They don't have time to develop rinds or strong aromas, so expect pure, dairy notes, but there can also be citrus, yogurt, and grassy flavours.

Examples: halloumi, ricotta, feta, mozzarella, burrata, paneer, cottage cheese.

Mould ripened
Cheesemakers sometimes age soft cheeses in their maturing rooms so that they develop bloomy or wrinkly coats. These white rinds are actually made up of edible moulds or yeasts that slowly break down the interior (the paste) underneath, until it is oozy and gooey, creating earthy, mushroomy and spicy notes.

Examples: Baron Bigod, Tunworth, Brie, Camembert, crottin, Brillat-Savarin.

Semi-hard
A big category that can be split into two main types – those with a crumbly texture and those with a springy texture. The former is a classic British style, while the latter is more common in continental Europe. Typically these cheeses are aged for weeks and months rather than years and the range of flavours is equally diverse, from savoury and tangy to earthy and caramel.

Examples: Cheshire, Wensleydale, Cornish Yarg (all crumbly); Tomme de Savoie, St Nectaire, Fontina (all springy).

Hard
By removing much of the whey from the curd during cheesemaking, larger, harder cheeses can be made. These can be aged for years, during which time they develop complex flavours, such as umami, roasted nuts and animal notes.

Examples: Cheddar, red Leicester, Manchego, Gouda, pecorino, double Gloucester.

Hard cooked
Often made in mighty wheels and drums (Emmenthal can weigh over 100kg/220lb), these cheeses are so called because of how they are made. The curd is cut very small and "cooked" (heated to over 50°C/120°F) to expel moisture so that huge cheeses can be created and aged for a long time. Sometimes called "Alpines", because many originate in the Alps, they are often sweet, nutty and crystalline.

Examples: Gruyère, Comté, bergkäse, Emmenthal, Parmigiano Reggiano, Grana Padano.

Blue
Penicillium roqueforti is what puts the blue into blue cheese. Added to the milk during cheesemaking, the mould grows within soft and crumbly cheeses as they mature, creating beautiful blue veins and fruity and peppery flavours.

Examples: Stilton, Stichelton, Cote Hill Blue, Roquefort, Gorgonzola, Rogue River Blue.

Washed rind
More magic in the maturing room. Cheeses are smeared (AKA "washed") with brine or a mixture of brine and alcohol to develop a pungent orange rind that brings meaty, smoky and funky notes to the cheese.

Examples: Stinking Bishop, Rollright, Epoisses, Langres, Taleggio, reblochon, Mont d'Or.

A word on flavoured cheeses
Any of the cheeses above can be taken in new directions with other flavours. Adding dried fruit, spices or other ingredients is a common tactic. Wensleydale with cranberries or truffled Brie are two of the best known. But cheeses can also be smoked, soaked in alcohol and wrapped in leaves or herbs.

Gr

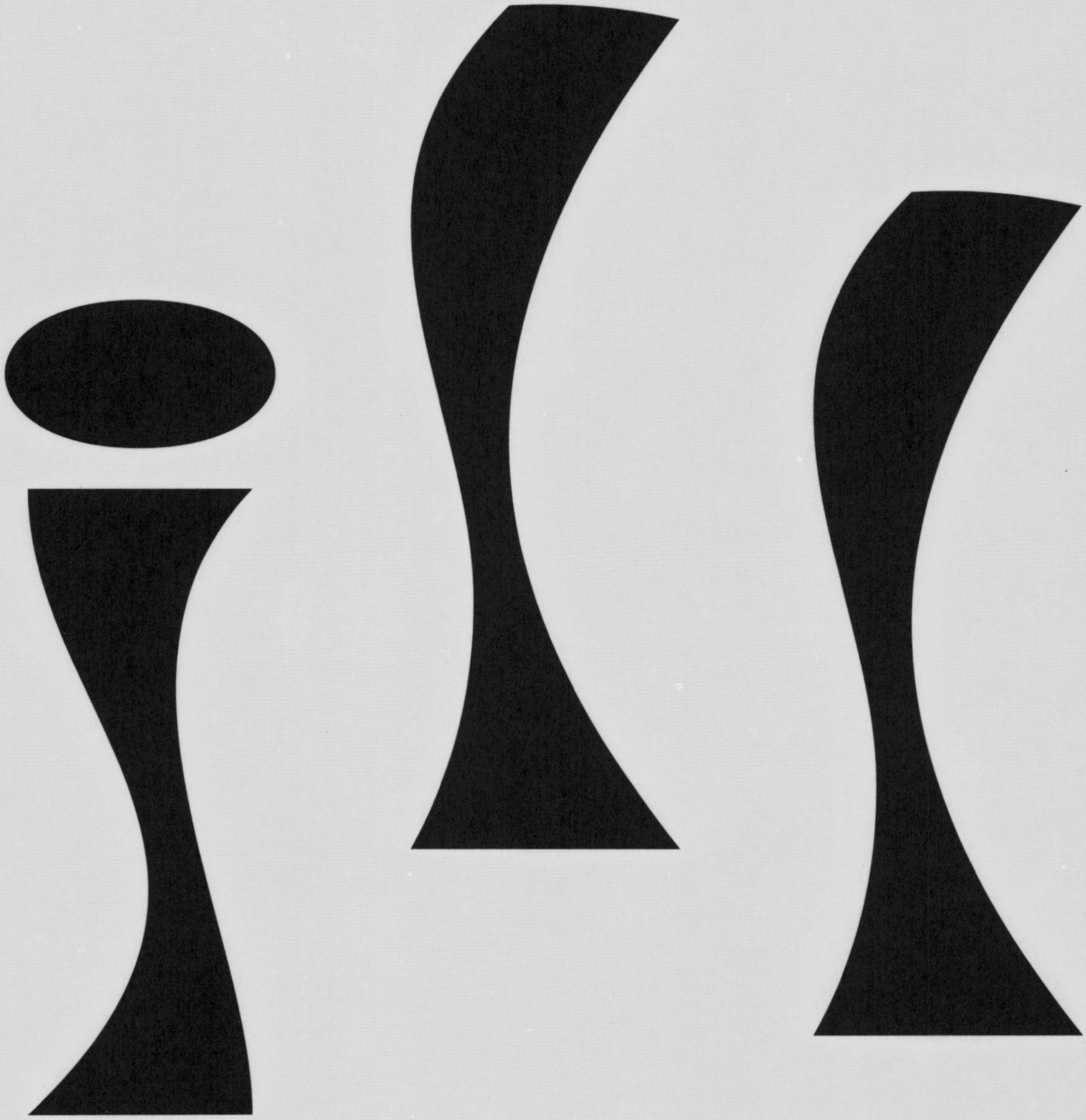

COOKING THE PERFECT GRILLED CHEESE

Why is it called a grilled cheese sandwich or just a "grilled cheese"? Isn't it a toastie? Okay, so yes, they are similar. In fact, the components are often identical.

But there are a few big differences. Toasties are made in toastie makers, which pinch the edges of the bread together so that they have closed sides. Grilled cheese sandwiches have open sides and are cooked on a grill, so are basically fried.

I'm being pedantic, but when you've devoted your life to wrangling molten cheese, these things matter. So how do you make irresistible grilled cheese sandwiches just like The Cheese Truck?

Let's start with the basics.

The bread

You'll need good-quality bread. We use sourdough at The Cheese Truck, but I'm not a bread snob. If your local bakery makes a good loaf using baker's yeast without lots of additives and processing aids, then that could work, too. Pre-packaged sliced bread that you find in supermarkets is not ideal. It has a pappy, cotton wool texture, which will likely fall apart when you're cooking.

The inside of a loaf is called the crumb. You want the crumb to be firm and consistent and not full of big air holes. Holey sourdough is fine if you're making eggs on toast, but when you're using it as a vessel to carry hot melted cheese to your mouth, those holes are going to leak everywhere.

I like flavour in my loaf, so I recommend something with a bit of rye or wholegrain flour. White bread lacks depth. It can also brown too quickly without developing a chewy, golden crust.

It might sound counter-intuitive, but bread that is a couple of days old and slightly stale is ideal. It has less moisture and will brown a lot more easily. The stiffness also helps with sandwich assembly.

The thickness of the slice is all important. There is nothing worse than when you get a grilled cheese made from two doorstop-thick slices. All you taste is bread. The cheese is lost. And it's the cheese that should take centre stage. Always.

We've always used a 12mm (½-inch) thick slice. It's the perfect compromise between structural integrity and creating a golden ratio of cheese to bread.

The cheese

Hard or semi-hard cheeses are usually your best bet. And make sure you pick ones with good meltability. Cheddar, Cheshire, Gouda and Alpine cheeses, such as Gruyère, all fit the bill. Raclette-style cheeses, such as Ogleshield, are also magnificent melters. Mozzarella can be a bit too wet for grilled cheese sandwiches, so look for low-moisture cooking mozzarella or unsmoked scamorza – a mozzarella-style cheese that is aged, so is a bit drier.

You can use other soft cheeses, but they are more likely to leak during cooking, which is a bit sad (and messy). The exceptions are soft and fluffy goats' cheeses, which sit in the sandwich rather well, going almost marshmallow-like in texture.

Mixing up different cheeses with contrasting characteristics is genius. For example, using Cheddar for its strong flavour with raclette for its stringy properties. Or contrasting a strong blue cheese with mozzarella to mellow out some of that punchiness.

When it comes to quantity, don't be tight. We're here because we love cheese, so don't skimp on the filling. If you're not putting in at least a minimum of 90g (3¼oz) of cheese per sandwich, then we can't be friends.

It goes without saying, but simplicity in cooking only works when the ingredients are the very best you can afford. So, put down that supermarket block Cheddar and get some proper cloth-bound farmhouse cheese instead. (See page 15 for what makes good cheese.)

Cooking technique

You probably don't have a flat-top griddle in your kitchen, which means the next best way to cook the perfect grilled cheese is in a frying pan.

A solid, heavy-bottomed pan is the ideal. Something that will offer a consistent heat throughout the base.

Place it over a low-medium heat and cook the sandwich for around 3–4 minutes on each side.

Once one side is done, flip the sandwich and apply weight to it. The best way to do this is with another pan and something heavy and heatproof: a can of baked beans or soup works pretty well. Applying pressure with a spatula or fish slice will also work.

When the time is up, check the outside of your sandwich is golden brown and crispy. Then check the cheese is fully melted. If not, give it a flip and fry for another minute.

When you reach oozing, golden perfection, flip the sandwich out of the pan and cut it in half.

It's best to leave your grilled cheese to rest for a couple of minutes before tucking in. This is a challenge, I'll admit, but when cheese is as hot as the sun, it's difficult to fully appreciate the flavour. Give it a moment to settle and you'll appreciate the cheese more.

Three golden rules

Keep it simple!
Your grilled cheese should be a celebration of your chosen cheese or cheeses. Allow them to shine. Pick a minimal number of filling ingredients that add contrast or enhance the experience. Don't go layering up random bits and bobs in that sandwich!

Butter all the way to the edges!
Slapdash buttering has no place here. Care should be taken that you coat every single millimetre of each slice of bread in delicious, melted butter. Any surface left unbuttered is going to burn instead of going golden brown and crisp.

Go low and slow!
Patience is a virtue. If you rush cooking a grilled cheese you will end up with burned bread or un-melted cheese. Both are absolute fails! You're looking for a perfectly golden and crisp outer crust and glossy rivers of cheese.

RECIPE FUNDAMENTALS

The irresistible grilled cheese sandwich is the dish that started our business. Would we be here now without those perfectly crisp slices of bread and delicious gooey cheese filling? Maybe not.

The following pages are crammed with some outstanding recipes, which are easy to make, perfect for sharing and great when you're too hungover to move.

They're here to give you initial starting points, but feel free to use creative freedom and add and take away ingredients as you see fit.

The basic recipe steps for a grilled cheese are below. Then in each following recipe we will just give some tips on sandwich assembly.

All these recipes make 2 hefty sandwiches.

• Melt the butter in a pan over a low–medium heat.

• Lay out your 4 slices of bread and brush the melted butter onto one side of all the slices. Flip the slices over and assemble the filling on 2 of the UNBUTTERED sides. Place the other slice of bread on top with the butter on the outside. Time to take it to the pan!

• Place the sandwiches in the pan. Cook for 3–4 minutes, applying pressure to the top of the sandwiches using a spatula or fish slice (or see opposite) while they are cooking, as this will help the cheese to melt.

• Flip the sandwiches over and cook on the other side for another 3–4 minutes.

• When both sides are golden brown and the cheese is oozing out, you're done!

Cheddar, raclette & onion

50g (1¾oz) salted butter

4 sourdough bread slices

140g (5oz) Cheddar cheese, grated (see note)

100g (3½oz) Ogleshield cheese (or use raclette), grated

¼ red onion, thinly sliced

¼ yellow onion, thinly sliced

The year is 1983. You're 23 years old. You walk into the Haçienda in Manchester and New Order are playing live. The sound of Blue Monday is powering through the speakers across the dancefloor. Your first time hearing this STONE-COLD CLASSIC.

It's sometimes easy to underappreciate the magnitude of a song, or a dish for that matter, when it becomes so iconic. But a Cheddar grilled cheese sandwich is just that: iconic.

Yes, it's simple. Yes, it's flogged just about everywhere, from service stations to fine dining restaurants. But when it's done right, that first bite is like hearing the opening drum beat to Blue Monday.

• Melt the butter in a pan, then butter the bread.

• Mix the two cheeses together and add the mixture to two slices of the bread: cup the cheese in your hands and press it into a sort of rugby ball shape, then push this down onto the slice. This ensures you get a decent amount of cheese on each slice, and it doesn't all trickle away when you move the sandwich to the pan.

• Next up, add your sliced onions. We always add a decent layer to the top of the cheese. No one cares about your breath when you're eating this, so don't skimp, if that's what you're worried about.

• Top with the other two slices, ensuring the buttered side is on top, then cook in a pan as on page 29. This is great served with pickled cucumbers (page 176) or cornichons.

Note: We use clothbound mature cheddars, such as Keen's from Somerset or Quicke's from Devon.

DRINKS PAIRING • DRINKS PAIRING • DRINKS PAIRING • DRINKS PAIRING •

Medium-dry cider

The sweetness of (hard) cider contrasts with the tang of Cheddar, while the acidity cuts through the creaminess.

Brie & mushroom duxelles

50g (1¾oz) salted butter

4 sourdough bread slices

160g (5¾oz) Mushroom duxelles (see page 169)

220g (8oz) young Brie cheese, sliced (see note)

Mushroom duxelles is a thing of French beauty. Up there with potato dauphinoise, onion soup and beef bourguignon! It's famous as a key part of beef Wellington, but on its own it also dovetails beautifully with earthy Brie.

• Melt the butter in a pan, then butter the bread.

• Divide the mushroom duxelles between two of the slices of bread, followed by the Brie.

• Top with the other two slices, ensuring the buttered side is on top, then fry as on page 29.

Note: We use Baron Bigod Brie from Suffolk. If you can't get it, then Brie de Meaux, Tunworth, Moses Sleeper or Camembert are fine alternatives.

Lancashire, chorizo & jalapeño salsa

FOR THE JALAPEÑO SALSA

Makes enough for 10 sandwiches, and will keep in the fridge for a week

8 jalapeños, stalks removed, deseeded and roughly chopped

½ yellow onion, roughly sliced

½ red onion, roughly sliced

4 garlic cloves

2 pinches of salt

juice of 2 limes

1 bunch of coriander (cilantro)

FOR THE SANDWICHES

50g (1¾oz) salted butter

4 sourdough bread slices

130g (4½oz) Lancashire cheese, grated

90g (3¼oz) unsmoked scamorza or cooking mozzarella cheese, grated

4 cooking chorizos (50-60g/1¾-2oz each), cooked and sliced in half lengthways

70g (2½oz) jalapeño salsa

This recipe is a variation on a classic from the truck. We used to use an elastic Mexican-style cheese made in Peckham by our good friend Kristen called Queso Chihuahua (named after the region in Mexico, not the dog). But it works just as well with crumbly Lancashire and added mozzarella for extra stringiness.

• To make the salsa, add all the ingredients to a blender and pulse until you have the consistency of a chunky salsa.

• To make the sandwiches, melt the butter in a pan, then butter the bread.

• Mix the two grated cheeses together in a bowl.

• Split the cheese between two slices of bread (using the rugby ball technique, see page 31).

• Add the chorizo and jalapeño salsa to taste on top of the cheese on each slice of bread. Top with the other two slices, ensuring the buttered side is on top, then fry as on page 29.

Note: You want a drier "cooking mozzarella" for a stringy melt. Unsmoked scamorza – an aged mozzarella-style cheese – is a great alternative (see page 39 for more). If you can't find Lancashire, then other crumbly British cheeses, such as Cheshire or Wensleydale, are good substitutes.

Beauvale, beef & honey

50g (1¾oz) salted butter

4 sourdough bread slices

80g (3oz) Beauvale cheese (Gorgonzola Dolce, Cote Hill Blue or Cambozola are good alternatives), broken into pieces

40g (1½oz) salt beef or pastrami

1½ tablespoons honey

Beauvale is Britain's answer to Gorgonzola – buttery, bulging and blue! We pair it with salt beef and honey for a proper indulgent grilled cheese sandwich that's sweet, savoury and creamy all at the same time. You can substitute the Beauvale for any squidgy, mild blue cheese. Just don't skimp on the honey!

· Melt the butter in a pan, then butter the bread.

· Split the Beauvale between two slices of bread. Add half the salt beef or pastrami and half the honey to each slice.

· Top with the other two slices of bread, ensuring the buttered side is on top, then fry as on page 29.

Red Leicester, ham & chilli jam

50g (1¾oz) salted butter

4 sourdough bread slices

2 thick-cut slices of good-quality ham

60g (2¼oz) Chilli jam (see page 164 or use shop bought; Tracklements Fresh Chilli Jam is great)

200g (7oz) red Leicester cheese, grated

There's only one farmhouse producer of red Leicester left in Leicestershire, and we would urge you to track them down. Sparkenhoe Red Leicester is cloth-bound and made with raw milk in the traditional manner with a soulful, savoury flavour and flaky texture.

Interesting fact: red Leicester gets its vibrant sunset colour from the addition of an edible vegetable dye called annatto, which comes from a seed grown in Central and South America. It has been added to cheese for hundreds of years to make it stand out on counters.

· Melt the butter in a pan, then butter the bread.

· Lay a slice of ham on each of two slices of bread.

· Next, add half the chilli jam to each followed by half of the red Leicester (use the rugby ball technique, see page 31).

· Top with the other two slices, ensuring the buttered side is on top, then fry as on page 29.

The beastie boy

FOR THE BBQ SAUCE

Makes 250ml (8½fl oz)

200g (7oz) tomato ketchup

1 tablespoon black treacle

1 teaspoon smoked paprika

25ml (1fl oz) cider vinegar

1 teaspoon honey

1 teaspoon English mustard

1 teaspoon onion powder

2 teaspoons hot sauce

FOR THE SANDWICH

50g (1¾oz) salted butter, melted

4 bread slices

120g (4¼oz) cooked macaroni
(around 55g/2oz dried macaroni)

120g (4¼oz) bechamel sauce
(from Five cheese macaroni,
see page 107)

80g (3oz) cooking mozzarella
or unsmoked scamorza cheese,
grated

1 quantity Roasted pineapple
(see page 176)

4 tablespoons BBQ Sauce

Back in 2018 we were invited to cater at the launch of the Beastie Boys' memoir at Rough Trade Records. It's an outstanding book full of essays, photos and cartoons, as well as recipes from legendary US chef Roy Choi. For the event we were asked to come up with a version of his grilled cheese sandwich from the book.

We adapted it quite a lot and made it our own, and it's had a cult following ever since. Release your inner Beastie!

To make the BBQ sauce

· Combine all the ingredients in a pan and bring to a simmer. Reduce the heat and simmer until thickened. The sauce can be stored in an airtight container in the refrigerator for up to 2 weeks.

To make the sandwiches

· Butter all the slices of bread and place them butter side down on a chopping board. Assemble the sandwiches: in a bowl mix the cooked macaroni, bechamel and mozzarella together. Split the mixture between two of the slices of bread, then add a layer of roasted pineapple followed by the BBQ sauce.

· Top with the other two slices, ensuring the buttered side is on top, then cook in a pan as on page 29.

SONG PAIRING · SONG PAIRING · SONG PAIRING · SONG PAIRING ·

No Sleep Till Brooklyn
BEASTIE BOYS

Licensed to Grill.

Goats' cheese, honey & walnut

50g (1¾oz) salted butter

leaves from 2 rosemary sprigs, finely chopped

4 sourdough bread slices

180g (6½oz) soft goats' cheese

40g (1½oz) walnut pieces

3 tablespoons honey

Lots of people claim they don't like goats' cheese, but this sandwich will convert them!

The secret is to get the right balance of flavours. The amount of honey is crucial. Take the recipe below as a guideline, but don't be afraid to add a little more honey if your cheese is more mature or has a stronger, more "goaty" taste to it. We use Rosary, made by Chris and Clare Moody in Wiltshire. But any fresh goats' cheese without a rind will do. The softer and creamier the better.

- Melt the butter in a pan. Add the rosemary leaves to the melted butter and simmer over a low heat for 5 minutes until the butter begins to turn a light shade of green. This means the rosemary is doing its job and imparting its flavour.

- Using a pastry brush, butter the outside of each slice of bread with the melted rosemary butter, leaving nothing in the pan.

- Flip over two of the slices of bread and spread the goats' cheese across them in a nice thick layer, then add the walnuts and drizzle with the honey.

- Top with the other two slices, ensuring the buttered side is on top, then fry as on page 29.

Sparkling Vouvray

Lemony and floral with refreshing bubbles.

Stilton, bacon & pear chutney

50g (1¾oz) salted butter

4 sourdough bread slices

4 smoked streaky (lean) bacon rashers, cooked

100g (3½oz) pear chutney (Dorset Blue Woodbridge Chutney is our fave)

180g (6½oz) Stilton cheese, sliced

2 gherkins (pickles), to garnish (optional)

This sandwich has been on the menu since day dot, even though it's not the most favoured among hungover festival revellers. Stilton isn't always the first choice when people are feeling fragile. However, it's unbelievably delicious. The perfect balance of salty and sweet.

We've always used Cropwell Bishop, but also highly recommend Colston Bassett. (See page 79 for more on blue cheese.)

- Melt the butter in a pan, then butter the bread.

- Lay out the bacon rashers across two of the slices of bread. Spread the chutney evenly on top – it should be sandwiched between the bacon and the cheese, so it doesn't make the bread soggy.

- Take half the cheese and place it on top of the chutney, then repeat with the second sandwich.

- Top them with the other two slices, ensuring the buttered side is on top, then fry as on page 29.

- Once cooked, cut in half, stack and serve with a gherkin (pickle) on the side. The crunch and acidity are a lovely contrast.

Corra Linn, broccoli, lemon & hazelnut

140g (5oz) longstem broccoli (broccolini)

olive oil

50g (1¾oz) salted butter

4 sourdough bread slices

200g (7oz) Corra Linn cheese (or other hard sheep's milk cheese), grated

30g (1oz) hazelnuts, crushed

1 lemon

The Errington family has been an integral part of reviving artisan cheesemaking in Scotland since the 1980s. Their hard sheep's milk cheese Corra Linn sits somewhere between a Cheddar and Manchego with complex flavours that are fruity, hazelnutty and brothy. If you can't find Corra Linn, then substitute with other hard, aged sheep's milk cheeses such as Manchego or pecorino.

- Preheat the oven to 180°C (350°F), Gas Mark 4.

- Toss the broccoli in olive oil and place on a tray. Roast in the oven for 12–15 minutes until tender and charred.

- Melt the butter in a pan, then butter the bread.

- Next, add half the Corra Linn to each of two slices of the bread (using the rugby ball technique, see page 31) along with half the broccoli and half the hazelnuts. Finish by giving each sandwich a good squeeze of lemon. Top with the other two slices of bread, ensuring the buttered side is on top, then fry as on page 29.

Mozzarella, bacon & chilli honey

50g (1¾oz) salted butter

4 sourdough bread slices

200g (7oz) cooking mozzarella or unsmoked scamorza cheese, grated (see below)

3 tablespoons Chilli honey (see page 85), or to taste (we usually serve some on the side for dipping)

4 smoked streaky (lean) bacon rashers, cooked

This sandwich is a guaranteed crowd pleaser. What's not to love about the holy trinity of stringy cheese, bacon and chilli honey? If you're feeling a bit fancy and want some spice, then swap out the bacon for 'nduja.

• Melt the butter in a pan, then butter the bread.

• Evenly distribute the mozzarella over two of the slices of bread.

• Drizzle the chilli honey over the mozzarella, coating the cheese, then place the bacon on top.

• Top with the other two slices, ensuring the buttered side is on top, then fry as on page 29.

Mozzarella

There's something hypnotic about watching mozzarella being made by hand. Fresh curd is plunged into hot water and then stretched and twirled by the cheesemaker until it develops its famous silky texture. That's when little spheres of the cheese are twisted off to make individual balls of mozzarella ("mozzare" means to "cut off" in Italian), which are popped into pots or bags of brine to stop them drying out.

The supple curd can also be shaped into bocconcini (bite-sized balls), ciliegine (cherry tomato-sized) and treccia (braided). There's also burrata – a mozzarella pouch filled with cream and scraps of cheese, which flows like lava when you cut into it. And you can smoke and age mozzarella to make cheeses, such as pear-shaped scamorza. They are all part of a family of *formaggi* known as "pasta filata" ("spun paste") because of the rhythmic spinning and stretching of the curd during production.

For salads and starters, rich buffalo mozzarella is best. The high butterfat content makes it so soft and silky that it dribbles down your chin. Mozzarella di Bufala Campana, a protected cheese made in southern Italy, is the original, but there are also British buffalo mozzarellas, such as Buffalicious and Laverstoke.

For cooking, slightly drier mozzarella, made with cows' milk ("fior de latte"), is often preferred because it melts better. It's known as "low moisture mozzarella" in the trade and melts into a cat's cradle of stringy strands on pizzas and mozzarella sticks. Scamorza is also good for cooking because it has been aged for a few weeks so is drier.

The best buffalo mozzarella has a thin, tight skin with an elastic heart that is neither soft nor rubbery. Sweet, milky and with a lactic tang, it's a wonderful creamy carrier of other flavours. Just add olive oil, tomatoes and basil.

Mike Thomson

Cheesemaker

Mike's Fancy Cheese, Belfast

The story of how Mike Thomson ended up making Northern Ireland's only raw milk cheese starts with him sleeping in a clapped out Hyundai Accent.

"I was doing a social work degree in Belfast, but academia wasn't for me," he explains. "I dropped out but still had my student loans and bursaries, so I used them to go on a road trip in my grandad's old car. I travelled around England and Wales sleeping in my car, meeting people and thinking of myself as a bit of troubadour. When I got back I had to pay it all back, so I got a job at a deli called Arcadia."

The deli was home to an excellent cheese counter, where Mike's interest was first kindled. He started a cheese blog and eventually ended up learning how to make cheese at the School of Artisan Food in Nottinghamshire, before making Sparkenhoe red Leicester.. He returned to Belfast in 2013 and set up his own business through a crowdfunding scheme.

Based in Newtownards on the outskirts of the city, Mike's Fancy Cheese makes a creamy, spicy, Stilton-style blue called Young Buck, using raw milk from a nearby farm. "I find this kind of cheese really pleasurable to make," he says. "Cheddars are big and noisy – there's lots of cutting and heating and stirring – and soft cheeses are small and fiddly. But Young Buck is 8kg (18lb) so it's just the right size for lifting and turning, and it only needs ageing for three months, which means we get paid sooner."

A typical day starts before dawn with curd from the previous shift salted and packed into moulds, before it's off to the farm to pick up the fresh milk. It's in the vat by 8.30am and cheesemaking finishes by mid-afternoon.

"We ladle the curd by hand from the vat onto a draining table, which takes a lot of twisting and leaning. It's a great work-out for your abs. We also use our hands and arms to break up the curd for salting. If you haven't done it for a while, you really feel the burn in your forearms."

The cheese is sold to local delis and restaurants, as well as cheesemongers in the Republic of Ireland and mainland Britain. Mike also has his own shop in Belfast, where he sells plenty of his own and other artisan cheeses.

"I love the simplicity of cheese. We buy milk from a local farm, make the cheese and sell it in Belfast eight miles away. It's straightforward and honest."

Tayler Carver

Sandwich queen

The Cheese Truck, London

What's the secret to making the ultimate grilled cheese sandwich? Well, using fantastic cheese is the obvious answer, but Tayler Carver has another tip: make sure you butter the outside of the bread all the way to the crusts. "If you don't, you end up with burned bits where there's no butter," she says.

Tayler should know. She's spent many summers working at a hot griddle in the back of a bright yellow converted ice-cream van, cooking thousands of grilled cheese sandwiches. at music festivals and street food markets.

"The genius of a grilled cheese sandwich is that they work at any time of the day – breakfast, lunch, when you're drunk or when you're stumbling back to your tent at 6am," says Tayler.

The Cheese Truck, nicknamed Archie, made its debut at Glastonbury in 2014, serving grilled sandwiches with British cheese from artisan producers such as Montgomery's Cheddar and Cropwell Bishop Stilton. They were so popular in 2015 that the truck served 12,000 sandwiches over the weekend.

"Glastonbury was a real baptism of fire," says Tayler. "I'd done a couple of markets, but this was 16-hour days and 20-metre queues. It was so hot, everything smelled of melted cheese including our clothes and hair – but we had a laugh. Obviously, when I wasn't on the grill I was out partying. I got by on about three hours of sleep a night."

The job was originally meant to be a stop-gap before Tayler took a job overseas, but the cheese life took hold and she's still with the business 9 years later. The following summer the business had two more trucks – Alfie and Audrey (Archie was lost to a crash and had to go to the crusher) – which they took to 26 festivals over three months.

"The ethos of the business really resonated with me," says Tayler. "We're about careful sourcing and good-quality produce. All the cheese we use comes from small producers. It's not about big dairy and mass-produced food."

Working on The Cheese Truck has also opened her eyes to the quality of British cheese. "I'm not on the griddle so much these days, more in the office, but I still eat a lot of cheese. I think it's pretty cool that we've got at least one thing coming out of the UK that we can be proud of."

Bloody Mary beans

Serves 4

drizzle of vegetable oil

½ celery stick, finely chopped

1 garlic clove, finely chopped

1 Scotch bonnet chilli, deseeded and finely chopped

800ml (1⅓ pints) tomato juice

1 tablespoon Worcestershire sauce

¼ teaspoon table salt

½ teaspoon black pepper

½ tablespoon celery salt

½ tablespoon tomato purée (paste)

1½ tablespoons cornflour (cornstarch), mixed with 50ml (2fl oz) cold water

800g (1lb 12oz) canned haricot (navy) beans, drained

If we had £1 for every time at 3am a drunk festival goer has asked us if these beans contain vodka, well we wouldn't be writing this book!

Anyway, this recipe doesn't contain cheese. But bear with us. It is the PERFECT accompaniment for a grilled cheese sandwich. Dip and enjoy! At festivals we sell these beans with a Cheddar and bacon grilled cheese sandwich, and it's widely regarded as lifesaving after a night on the sauce.

- In a medium saucepan, heat the vegetable oil over a medium heat. Add the celery, garlic and Scotch bonnet and fry for 30 seconds until softened.

- Add the tomato juice, Worcestershire sauce, salt, black pepper, celery salt and tomato purée (paste). Cook over a medium heat for 20 minutes until slightly reduced.

- Add the cornflour (cornstarch) and water mixture and cook for 1 minute until slightly thickened.

- Add the drained haricot (navy) beans and gently simmer for 10 minutes until the beans are softened and cooked through.

- These will keep in an airtight container in the refrigerator for up to 5 days, and will only get better in flavour.

Apple & habanero hot sauce

Makes approx. 350ml (12fl oz)

125g (4½oz) cooking apples, peeled, cored and roughly chopped

35g (1¼oz) habanero or Scotch bonnet chillies, deseeded, stalks removed and roughly chopped

60g (2¼oz) mild red chillies, stalks removed and roughly chopped

½ small yellow onion, roughly chopped

thumb-sized piece of fresh root ginger, peeled and roughly chopped

½ teaspoon ground allspice

1 garlic clove

3 tablespoons malt vinegar

85ml (3fl oz) water

1 teaspoon table salt

½ teaspoon sugar

100ml (3½fl oz) apple juice

Hot sauces should have flavour, not just intense heat, and this recipe has just that. It treads a fine line between warming and hot. It's also the perfect partner to our cauliflower cheese fritters (see page 143).

· Add all the ingredients except the apple juice to a saucepan over a medium heat and bring to a simmer.

· Cook until the apple, chillies and onion have gone soft, and the liquid has slightly reduced. This should take around 20 minutes.

· Remove from the heat and allow to cool for 10 minutes.

· Transfer to a blender or food processor and blend until smooth, then add the apple juice.

· It will keep in an airtight container in the refrigerator for up to 1 week.

House tomato ketchup

Makes approx. 275ml (9½fl oz)

4 teaspoons vegetable oil

1 yellow onion, thinly sliced

75g (2¾oz) demerara (turbinado) sugar

1 teaspoon ground coriander

½ teaspoon black pepper

¼ star anise

175ml (6fl oz) passata (puréed canned tomatoes)

200g (7oz) canned chopped tomatoes

50ml (2fl oz) white wine vinegar

When you spend time and effort sourcing the most delicious cheeses in the UK and then put a lot of love into creating dishes that let their flavour shine, it's a bit heartbreaking to see people slathering Tommy K all over them.

But we're realists. People like ketchup. We get that. So we decided to come up with our own ketchup recipe. If you're going to douse your cheese in tomato sauce, make sure it's a tasty one.

- Heat the vegetable oil in a medium pan over a low heat. Add the onion and fry for 10 minutes until caramelized.

- Add the sugar, coriander, black pepper and star anise. Stir and leave over the heat for 1 minute for the flavours to develop.

- Add the rest of the ingredients and bring to the boil. Reduce to a simmer and cook for 30 minutes.

- Remove the star anise and transfer to a blender or food processor, then blend to a purée.

- Return the mix to the pan and put back over a medium heat for around 5 minutes to reduce the liquid. When at a ketchup-like consistency, take the sauce off the heat and check the seasoning, adding salt and pepper to taste.

- Place in an airtight container, leaving to cool before you seal. The ketchup will keep for 1 week in the refrigerator or 2 months in the freezer.

Three cheese & cider fondue fries

Serves 2

FOR THE FONDUE SAUCE

80g (3oz) Ogleshield cheese
(or use raclette), grated

80g (3oz) Cheddar cheese,
grated

80g (3oz) cooking mozzarella
or unsmoked scamorza cheese,
grated or finely diced

15g (½oz) cornflour (cornstarch)

pinch of nutmeg

pinch of salt

pinch of black pepper

140ml (⅓ pint) (hard) cider

splash of lemon juice

splash of Somerset cider brandy
(optional, but a nice touch;
Calvados works too)

TO SERVE

½ quantity (375g/13oz) Crispy
oven chips (see page 55)

pickled silverskin
(pearl or cocktail) onions

cornichons

Cheesy chips (fries) at festivals are often a real let down. A handful of grated cheese chucked on top of some fries is a crime against cheese and chips! When you come to The Cheese Truck you expect a little more than that, and of course we deliver. Enter our fondue fries…

This three cheese and cider fondue sauce, which rides atop our fries at festivals, is a game changer.

• To make the fondue sauce, mix together the Ogleshield, Cheddar, mozzarella, cornflour (cornstarch), nutmeg, salt and pepper in a bowl, until the cheese is all evenly coated.

• In a pan over a medium heat, bring the cider and lemon juice to the boil.

• Beat in the dry cheese mixture over a medium heat, continuously scraping the bottom of the pan so it doesn't stick.

• Keep stirring until the fondue is thick and smooth.

• Add the cider brandy, if using, and stir in.

• To serve, place the fries on a serving dish and top with the fondue sauce. Garnish with pickled onions and cornichons.

THE CHEESE WITH A SPLIT PERSONALITY

Cheddar is made everywhere, from Sydney to San Francisco. It's one of the world's most popular cheeses. But it's in the UK where its tangy charms are most cherished. Open a refrigerator in any British kitchen and you can almost guarantee it will contain a lump of the stuff. But not all Cheddars are created equal.

There's a radically different range of styles, made in completely different ways, that all bear the name "Cheddar". There's block, cloth-bound and "reformed" Cheddars, not to mention everything from mild to vintage and even goat and sheep's milk versions. In other words, there's Cheddar and then there's Cheddar, and then there's Cheddar.

Cloth-bound

On the southern edge of the Mendip Hills in Somerset is a village called Cheddar. It's famous for its limestone caves and for giving its name to Britain's most famous cheese, which has been made in the area since the twelfth century. There is still a cheesemaker in the village – the Cheddar Gorge Cheese Company, which makes cloth-bound cheeses and ages them in the nearby caves.

There would have once been thousands of these kinds of traditional Cheddar makers in Somerset and across the UK, but there are now just a handful left. Each of these last remaining Cheddars has its own unique flavour and texture that reflect the farm, dairy and maturing rooms where it is made.

Isle of Mull, for example, is made on the Hebridean island of the same name with raw milk from cows that are fed draff – spent barley grains left over from whisky production at the local distillery. Big and beefy with a mustardy and almost boozy tang, it's a very different beast to Quicke's Cheddar, which is made in the gentler climes of south Devon, where the cows graze lush West Country grass almost all year round. Quicke's often has a corresponding sweet, grassy note.

These cheeses are made by hand in open vats where the curd is drained and gathered into blocks, which are stacked on top of each other and turned. This piling process, called "Cheddaring", helps squeeze whey from the curd, build acidity and develop texture, before milling, salting and pressing into 25–27kg (55–60lb) cylinders called "truckles".

Many traditional Cheddar makers wrap their truckles in muslin cheesecloth soaked in lard to seal and protect the rind, before ageing for a year or more, during which time natural moulds grow on the cloth and the cheeses lose around 10% of their weight through evaporation. The cloth is removed (see photo overleaf) before the cheese is sold, although you can still see the imprint and smell a musty, bandage-like aroma on the rind.

There are lots of reasons why cloth-bound Cheddars are few and far between. One of the most important is the unstoppable rise of block Cheddar – a cheaper, factory version of Cheddar, which became ubiquitous in the twentieth century. Unlike other cheeses, such as Parmigiano Reggiano and Roquefort, the name "Cheddar" was never protected by law, which meant it spread from its West Country heartland to be made all over the world. Today, block Cheddar is a refrigerator staple not just in the UK, but also in the US, Canada, Ireland, New Zealand and Australia.

Made on automated lines that churn out thousands of tonnes of cheese a month, it is typically formed into 20kg (44lb) blocks, which are vacuum sealed in plastic before being aged. This is done to stop a rind forming, which means less wastage, and to stop evaporation. It's why even mature and extra mature cheeses still have a surprisingly soft and squidgy texture.

Block Cheddar is often much sweeter than traditional cheeses because of the use of a Swiss starter culture called *Lactobacillus helveticus*, which adds a fruity, candied flavour that the sweet-toothed public love. Sweet, creamy and salty, block Cheddar gives a lot of upfront flavour and has an appealing immediacy. It's also much cheaper than traditional Cheddars – a quarter of the price or even less.

Chocolate and wood chips

That's not where Cheddar ends, however. There are all sorts of other cheeses that call themselves Cheddar. Waxed Cheddars, which come in shapes from hockey pucks and hearts to stars and bricks, are made by taking block Cheddar and milling it into little pieces, which are then squished back together again using a machine called an extruder.

This squeezes the cheese through a mould to form a continuous cheese sausage in the desired shape, which can then be sliced into individual cheeses. Other ingredients can be added to these so called "reformed" cheeses during the process, from dried cranberries and chilli flakes to dried herbs and even chocolate chips, to make flavoured Cheddars. The less said about chocolate Cheddar the better.

Then there are Cheddars made with different types of milk. Sheep, goat and buffalo Cheddars are all available and have their own distinct personalities. There are also smoked versions, which are made with flavourings or by cold-smoking cheeses over smouldering wood chips.

How long Cheddar is kept in the maturing room has a huge impact. There are no legal definitions in the UK on what constitutes mild, medium, mature and extra mature, and some cheesemakers play fast and loose with the terms. But mild Cheddars, which are typically aged for just a couple of months, tend to be delicate and buttery, while mature Cheddars at a year old have more bite and intensity. Vintage Cheddars, aged for 18 months or more, are different again, with powerful umami notes creating an almost itchy sensation on the tongue.

In the end, the best way to navigate this confusing Cheddar maze is to taste as many as you can, and make up your own mind. Block and waxed Cheddars might be cheap, but they are often a quick fix. The sweet and salty hit soon wears off and you find yourself reaching for more cheese.

Traditional Cheddars have much greater depth, complexity and length. There really is nothing to compare to the firm, snappy texture and complex layers of flavour. They roll around your tongue and rumble on in your mind, taking in everything from grassy, earthy and buttery notes to roasted onions, horseradish and beef stock. Proper Cheddar might cost more, but that's because it's the real deal.

Truffled Brie burger

Serves 2

FOR THE PATTIES

Makes 2 x 175g (6oz) patties

340g (11¾oz) beef mince
(ground beef) – fat content
should be at least 20 per cent

salt and pepper

FOR THE TRUFFLE MAYO

Makes 550ml (1¼ pint)

1 egg yolk

1½ teaspoons wholegrain mustard

1½ teaspoons white wine vinegar

juice of ¼ lemon, or more to taste

2 teaspoons truffle paste (we use
minced black truffles from Truffle
Hunter), or more to taste

100ml (3½fl oz) truffle oil (we use
Truffle Hunter's White Truffle Oil)

400ml (14fl oz) vegetable oil

salt

FOR THE CARAMELIZED ONIONS

50ml (2fl oz) olive oil

2 large yellow onions, thinly sliced

salt

FOR THE BURGERS

vegetable oil, for greasing

2 burger buns

25g (1oz) salted butter, melted

140g (5oz) Brie cheese, cut into
thin slices

50g (1¾oz) Bacon jam
(see page 169)

salt and pepper

I never wanted a burger on the menu at our restaurant in Camden,
but our butcher sent us some burger mince by mistake one day.
We came up with this recipe at the last moment and it sold out
so quickly that it's not left the menu since.

**This recipe makes more mayo than you need, but it goes with
everything so it's worth having extra in the refrigerator.**

To make the patties
· Mix the beef and seasoning together in a bowl. Split the mixture into
  two and shape into balls. Then flatten with the palm of your hand until
  3cm (1-inch) thick. Place on a plate, cover with cling film (plastic wrap)
  and refrigerate for 30 minutes before cooking. Season the outsides
  just before cooking.

To make the truffle mayo
TIP: Make sure all the ingredients are at room temperature.

· Place all the ingredients, apart from the two oils and salt, in the bowl
  of a food processor or blender and blend together.

· Combine the truffle and veg oil in a jug and drizzle the mixture very
  slowly into the mixture as the food processor is running. If you rush
  this step, you risk splitting the mayonnaise.

· You're looking for a thick and creamy texture. If it's too stiff, add a few
  teaspoons of water to loosen. Add salt, more lemon juice and/or truffle
  paste according to your taste.

· Keep in an airtight container in the refrigerator for up to 5 days.

To make the caramelized onions
· Add the oil to a wide-based pan over a medium–high heat. Add the
  onions, then turn the heat down to low and cook, stirring regularly,
  for about 30 minutes, until brown and caramelized. Remove the pan
  from the heat.

To make the burgers
· Add a little oil to a heavy-bottomed frying pan and heat over a high
  heat until very hot.

· Add the patties to the pan and cook for around 5–6 minutes on each
  side for medium and 8–9 minutes on each side for well done (see tips).

Recipe continues overleaf

SONG PAIRING · SONG PAIRING · SONG PAIRING · SONG PAIRING · SONG PAIRING ·

Is It All Over My Face
LOOSE JOINTS

Yes, it most probably is!

- While they're cooking, slice your buns in half and give them a good brush of melted butter on the cut side. Add them, cut side down, to a second frying pan over a medium heat for 3-5 minutes to toast them.

- Once you've cooked the burgers on both sides, add the Brie on top of them. Add a splash of water to the pan and then quickly cover with a lid so the steam melts the cheese.

- When the buns are ready, remove them from the heat and spread the bottom buns with bacon jam. Then add a generous dollop of truffle mayonnaise to the top and bottoms of each bun.

- When the cheese has melted and the burgers are cooked, get them out of the pan and place one on the base of each bun.

- Return the pan to a medium heat; leave any remaining fat and juice from the burgers, as this will all add flavour. Add the caramelized onions and gently heat for 2-3 minutes while the burgers rest.

- Add the caramelized onions to the top of the burgers and finish with the top of the buns.

- Now tuck in and get messy. Plenty of kitchen roll is a must!

Top 5 burger tips

There are a few different ways you can cook burgers but we think they always cook best on a hot griddle or heavy-bottomed frying pan. Either way, here are our top tips for cooking them:

1. Keep the burgers cold until you're ready to cook them. Unlike other meat, they don't need to be brought to room temperature before hitting the heat.

2. Make it HOT. It doesn't matter if you're cooking on a grill, in a pan or whatever else. Just make sure it's hot before your burgers join the party. We're looking for that sizzle.

3. Flip them once and once only; this isn't pancake day! Let your burgers cook in peace and they'll return the favour with juicy, moist deliciousness.

4. Don't press them down; leave them be. If you apply pressure, you're only going to squeeze out all that juice and flavour.

5. Let them rest! Give your burgers a few minutes to rest after cooking to allow the juice to re-distribute through the patty. You can't rush these things.

Crispy oven chips

Serves 4

6 tablespoons vegetable oil

750g (1lb 10oz) Maris Piper (or Russet) potatoes, skin on and cut into 2cm (¾-inch) thick, chip-shaped batons (fries)

2½ tablespoons cornflour (cornstarch)

salt

Deep-fat fryers are few and far between these days, so we've put together a recipe for some cracking oven chips (fries) that are just waiting to be smothered in melted cheese.

• Preheat the oven to 200°C (400°F), Gas Mark 6.

• Place 5 tablespoons of the vegetable oil in a large, deep baking tray and place in the oven to preheat for 15 minutes until shimmering.

• Meanwhile, bring a large pan of salted water to a boil.

• Add the chips (fries) and boil for 3–5 minutes until the edges have just started to go soft. Drain in a colander and allow them to steam themselves dry for 10 minutes.

• Add the chips back to the pan and sprinkle with the remaining tablespoon of vegetable oil, the cornflour (cornstarch), and a couple of good pinches of salt. Shake! You want to get a good coverage of flour, oil and salt and to bash up the soft edges a bit. But be careful, as you don't want them falling apart.

• Carefully add the chips to the tray of hot oil and use a spatula to ensure they are all covered in oil. Arrange them in one layer and don't overcrowd the pan as they won't crisp up! Use two baking trays if necessary.

• Cook them in the oven for 15 minutes, then turn and cook for another 15 minutes. You're looking for perfectly golden and crispy chips.

• Check the seasoning, adding more salt if required, and serve straight away.

Lanark Blue & sherry rarebit

Serves 2

1 shallot, finely diced

150ml (5fl oz) cream sherry
(or tawny port)

175g (6oz) Lanark Blue cheese,
crumbled (or any punchy blue
cheese, see recipe introduction)

1 tablespoon crème fraîche

1 large (US extra-large) egg yolk

½ teaspoon English mustard

1½ teaspoons honey

10g (¼oz) walnuts, chopped

2 large sourdough bread slices

chicory (Belgian endive), endive
or frisée salad, to serve

Classic Welsh rarebit is usually made with Cheddar. But this recipe completely rips up the rule book by using Lanark Blue – a feisty sheep's blue from Scotland – and sherry to create a rich, indulgent version that is all its own. If you can't find cream sherry, then replace with tawny port. Likewise, any punchy sheep's blue cheese, such as Roquefort or Beenleigh Blue, can be used.

· Place the shallots in a pan, add the sherry and place over a medium heat. Cook for around 10 minutes until the sherry reduces to a thick syrup. Be careful not to take it too far and let the all the liquid evaporate.

· Preheat the grill (broiler) to 180°C (350°F).

· In a large bowl, place the Lanark Blue, crème fraîche, egg yolk, mustard, honey and walnuts. Add the cream sherry syrup and mix everything together well to form a thick paste.

· Toast your slices of bread (both sides), then spread the cheese mixture evenly across them.

· Place under the grill for a few minutes until molten and golden brown.

· Serve with a simple chicory (Belgian endive), endive or frisée salad.

TIME: THE SECRET INGREDIENT

Time slows down in a cheese maturing room. The clamour of the outside world is quickly forgotten in the cool, damp space where rows of cheeses sit quietly on wooden shelves for weeks, months and even years as they gradually ripen.

There's a serene stillness to these rooms, but linger a little longer and you soon become aware that life is all around. A pungent earthy aroma hangs in the air and there's an almost imperceptible sense of things growing.

Maturing rooms are not dead spaces. Far from it. They are filled with natural microbes that are slowly colonizing the cheeses. Over time, natural yeasts, moulds and bacteria grow on the rinds, creating complex flavours and textures.

In fact, you could argue that time is the secret ingredient of many great cheeses. In France they call cheese maturing "affinage", which translates as "refining". Specialist affineurs buy young cheeses from dairies and then nurture them in temperature- and humidity-controlled rooms until they reach their full potential.

Techniques, such as turning, brushing and washing the cheeses in brine, are also employed, while hard cheeses will periodically be tapped to listen for internal cracks that shouldn't be there. A long sharp tool, known as a cheese iron (cheese trier), is also plunged into the cheese so that a cross section can pulled out and checked to see how aroma, flavour and texture are developing.

Affinage has a long history in France, but also in Switzerland and Italy, where specialist maturers work their magic on soft, blue and washed-rind cheeses, as well as hard cheeses, such as Comté and Gruyère, which can be aged for over a year. Parmigiano Reggiano and Gouda are aged for even longer – two years or more.

Many affineurs have built their own specialist maturing rooms, but plenty still operate from traditional cellars and caves. Marcel Petite, one of the most respected affineurs of Comté, has a cathedral-like underground ageing facility in a former Napoleonic fort in the Jura mountains in France. And every round of Roquefort must, by law, be matured in the limestone caves of Roquefort-sur-Soulzon in the South of France, where the raw sheep's milk cheese has been matured for a thousand years.

The art of affinage

In the UK and US, cheesemakers and cheesemongers are also cottoning on to the improvements that affinage can bring to cheese. Many have travelled to France to take courses at affinage schools, and are now investing heavily in state-of-the-art maturation rooms (see page 92).

In Vermont in the US, Jasper Hill has built a remarkable series of maturing cellars deep beneath its farm near Greensboro. Resembling the secret lair of a James Bond villain (but with lots of cheese), the 2,000-sq-m (22,000-sq-ft) facility comprises a central hub, called the Ellipse, with seven climate-controlled vaults leading from it. Each is designed for different styles of cheese made by Jasper Hill and other small producers.

Vault 1 is the perfect environment for mould-ripened cheeses, such as Harbison – a soft and silky cheese encircled by a spruce band – while Vault 7 is high in humidity to encourage blue

veins of *Penicillium roqueforti* mould to spread throughout its peppery Bayley Hazen Blue.

British cheesemonger Neal's Yard Dairy has also invested in maturing rooms under railway arches in Bermondsey, south London. The high-ceilinged, brick vaults are the perfect place to recreate a cave-like atmosphere, with five rooms for cheeses ranging from cloth-bound Cheddars and Goudas to funky washed rinders, Bries and blues.

Tina the Turner

Somerset Cheddar-maker Westcombe Dairy has gone one step further and dug out 15,000 tonnes of soil from one of the hills on its farm to create a huge cave-like cellar in which to house hundreds of cloth-bound cheeses, which are stacked on wooden shelves that rise to the ceiling. The Cheddars develop a multi-coloured coat of moulds, which add to the final flavour of the cheese, and are brushed and turned regularly as they mature by a special robot, imported from Switzerland, christened Tina the Turner.

The appetite for affinage in the UK is such that an annual competition was launched by education organization the Academy of Cheese and Devon Cheddar-maker Quicke's in 2022.

The inaugural event involved 10 three-month-old Quicke's Cheddars, made on the same day, being sent to cheesemongers and makers across the UK, who matured them in different ways for a year.

The cheeses were reunited to be blind judged by a panel of experts at a final in London, and the results were remarkably different. While every truckle tasted like a Quicke's cheese, they each had their own unique characters in terms of flavour and texture, depending on how and where they had been matured.

The winning cheese, matured by Perry Wakeman at Cambridgeshire cheesemonger Rennet & Rind, was grassy, buttery and tangy with a long savoury finish. It was later revealed he had become so attached to the cheese that he had nicknamed it Priscilla. In the end she went the way of all good cheeses – cut into wedges to meet soaring demand from customers who wanted to taste the winning cheese.

It pays to take your time.

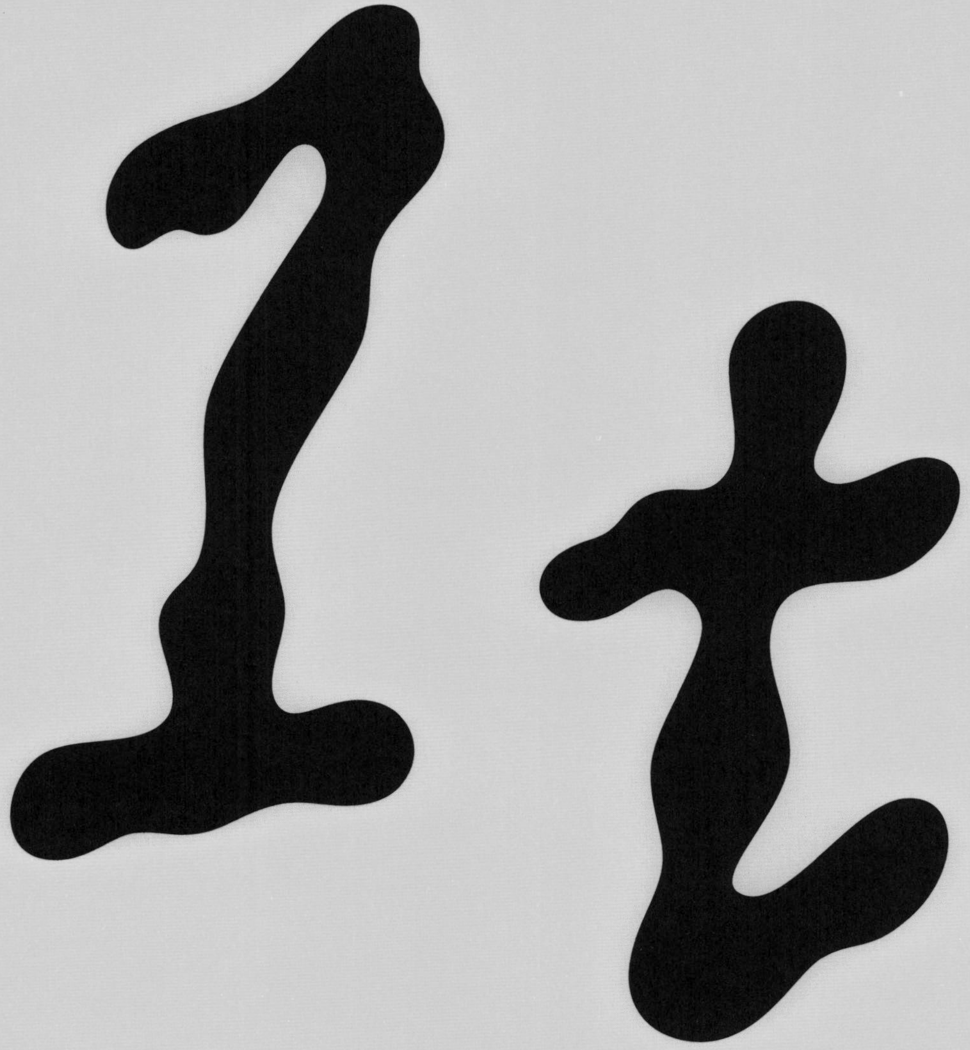

HOW TO FONDUE

In the UK, we tend to see fondue as a nostalgic cliché, reminiscent of the 1970s, or unwanted fondue sets for wedding presents. Well, I'm too young to remember the 70s, and sadly didn't get a fondue set as a wedding present, but you get my point.

The Swiss, on the other hand, take fondue SERIOUSLY. To them, it's more than just dunking some stale bread in a big old bowl of melted cheese – it's a full-on celebration meal with its own rules and etiquette. If we're going to do a fondue night at home, we're going to go all in, am I right?! So here are a few pointers to make your evening that bit more authentic.

Get set

It is possible to make fondue in a saucepan, but if you can't keep it warm at the table somehow, it is likely to split and/or congeal. So we would highly recommend buying a proper fondue set, comprising a pan, a stand, heater and the long forks you need for dipping. We use cast iron Staub pots in the restaurants, but Stöckli and Boska are also good brands.

Many fondue pots can be used with gas or induction hobs (check first) so you can make your fondue in the pot you are going to serve it in. Once it's ready, just transfer to the burner to keep it warm and melted at the table. Alternatively, make in a saucepan and pour into the pot over the burner.

Slow and low

The main thing is: DON'T BOIL THAT FONDUE. You don't want to see violently bubbling cheese. because you will make it less stringy.

Choose your cheese wisely. In Switzerland, Gruyère, Emmenthal and Vacherin Fribourgeois (a buttery, semi-soft cheese) are classic fondue cheeses because they melt so well. But Gouda-style cheeses and other hard and even crumbly cheeses can work well. The key is to pick cheeses with flavour.

The wine is also important. Choose a bone-dry white wine. The acidity stops the cheese from splitting.

Use your bread

The bread for dipping should be a day old and slightly stale. This is to enhance its sturdiness and ensure you're not dropping chunks in the fondue with every dip. (Read on to discover why.)

Chop your bread into cubes, ensuring you've got a nice chunk of crust on each cube. You'll want to pierce the crust with your fork to ensure it doesn't disintegrate in the pot – structural integrity, as an architect would call it!

There are plenty of other dippables. Use whatever takes your fancy! We're fans of cured meat or cooked vegetables like mushrooms, cauliflower and sprouts – pigs in blankets is a personal fave!

Easy on the tongue

Fondue is a communal meal. We're all dipping from the same pot, so let's try to think about what's going in there.

It's best to remove the bread from the fork with your front teeth. Being too tongue heavy or engulfing the bread and fork with your lips is not a good look.

If this is date night, then sass it up, but if you're eating with your folks or housemates, keep it respectful!

Stir it up

So, we'll start with the obvious one:
NO DOUBLE DIPPING.

Your fondue fork isn't only to get hot cheese into your mouth. It's also used to stir the fondue regularly, which helps to prevent the cheese from separating, or sticking and burning. So, with every dip, plunge that bread deep and stir in a figure of eight (apparently tradition as well), then bring it out of the cheese, hover for a minute to cool, and devour!

La religieuse

Now, if you've been following the guidelines above and stirring that fondue as you eat, and the fondue has been on a low bubble, you might find a little something special at the end: a golden crust of cheese on the bottom of the pot, known as *la religieuse* (because it resembles the cap of a nun).

Please, please, please don't waste this little cheese crust! It's one of the most delicious parts of the fondue. Grab a knife and prise it out, share it with your fellow diners and savour that cheesy heaven!

Don't lose your bread

There seem to be various forfeits for the person who manages to drop their bread in the pot, ranging from kissing everyone around the table, to paying for the meal or having a shot of kirsch.

I'm all into the idea of setting a forfeit before you start the meal, but I'm not going to tell you what that should be. Come up with some good ones while you're cooking your fondue.

Wine for the win

Now this is crucial and the easiest of the rules to get behind. The Swiss believe that drinking a dry, acidic white wine is key. The belief is that the alcohol in the wine aids digestion, and the acidity helps to refresh the palate and cut through all that cheese. It's almost medicinal!

The use of alcohol to aid digestion goes one step further in the traditional fondue eating experience, with a shot of kirsch cherry liqueur to finish the meal (or as a forfeit!). Truly the cherry on top.

If you're not into booze, then hot tea is also traditional with fondue. Cold soft drinks are generally a no-go, as they're believed to make the cheese coagulate. There's no real proof of this though, so if you fancy a cold drink, who are we to tell you otherwise?

Opposite we run you through the steps for cooking our Classic Four Cheese Fondue and dippables, then with the other fondue recipes we've just added any specific variations, leaving you to your own devices.

Classic four cheese fondue

Serves 2

FOR THE DIPPABLES

400g (14oz) new potatoes, halved

1 sourdough loaf, preferably
on the stale side

cornichons

salt and pepper

FOR THE FONDUE

90g (3¼oz) Cornish Kern cheese,
grated (or use Gruyère)

90g (3¼oz) Gouda cheese,
grated

90g (3¼oz) Ogleshield cheese,
grated (or use raclette)

90g (3¼oz) Mayfield cheese,
grated (or use Emmenthal)

8g (2 teaspoons) cornflour
(cornstarch)

1 garlic clove, halved

125ml (4fl oz) dry white wine (can
be substituted with apple juice)

juice of ½ lemon

nutmeg, for grating

STEP 1: To prepare the dippables
- Preheat the oven to 190°C (375°F), Gas Mark 5.

- Place the potatoes in a pan of cold salted water, ensuring they are covered. Bring to the boil and simmer for 10–15 minutes. Drain and season with salt and pepper until slightly al dente.

- Meanwhile, refresh your loaf: moisten the outside with a few tablespoons of water, and then bake in the oven for 10 minutes, until the crust is crispy. Slice into cubes small enough to fit in your mouth.

STEP 2: To prepare the fondue
- In a bowl, mix the grated cheeses with most (5g/1½ teaspoons) of the cornflour (cornstarch). Ensure the cheese is evenly coated.

- In a small bowl, mix your spare cornflour with a little cold water. Keep aside for later.

STEP 3: To prepare the pot
- Rub the cut edge of the garlic clove around the side and bottom of the pot, then crush the whole clove with the back of a knife and sling it in.

- Add the white wine to the pot with the lemon juice. Then grate in a decent pinch of nutmeg (to taste).

- Place the pot over a medium heat on the hob and bring to the boil.

STEP 4: To make the fondue
- Reduce the heat, so the mixture stops boiling. Add your cheese to the wine, a handful at a time, and whisk HARD after each handful, allowing the cheese to fully melt before adding more. Don't let the cheese boil.

- Once all the cheese is added, give the fondue a good whisk until it has all melted and it is glossy, smooth and stringy. If it starts to split, or you're not getting a smooth fondue, then add a little of your cornflour–cold water mixture and WHISK!

- Leave over a low heat while you complete the next steps.

STEP 5: To serve
- Plate up your bread, potatoes, cornichons and any other accompaniments you fancy. If you haven't already, assemble your fondue burner (making sure it's on a flat, heatproof surface!) and light it up.

- Ceremoniously deliver the pot of fondue to the table and ENJOY!

DRINKS PAIRING · DRINKS PAIRING · DRINKS PAIRING · DRINKS PAIRING ·

Chablis

Bone-dry, steely
and sophisticated
– a classy way to cut
through the goo.

Goats' cheese fondue

200g (7oz) semi-hard goats' cheese, rind removed and grated (we use Killeen Goat Gouda)

100g (3½oz) fresh goats' cheese, crumbled (we use Rosary goats' cheese)

8g (2 teaspoons) cornflour (cornstarch)

1 garlic clove, halved

60ml (4 tablespoons) double (heavy) cream

60ml (4 tablespoons) dry white wine

1 teaspoon lemon juice

finely chopped chives, to garnish

Five years ago we went on a very serious research trip to the Alps. The aim was to eat fondue for three days and find some inspiration for our upcoming Fondue Thursday nights. It's a hard life!

We tried a goats' cheese fondue that blew all our minds. We'd never thought about using goats' cheese in a fondue, but it was probably our favourite dish of the trip. We came up with our own version as soon as we got back.

• Place both cheeses into a bowl and mix together. Add the cornflour (cornstarch) and toss, ensuring the cheese is evenly coated.

• Scrape the garlic around the base of your fondue pot and then add to the pot with the cream, wine and lemon juice.

• Bring this up to a simmer, then reduce the heat and add the cheese mix.

• Whisk gently until the cheese is just over half melted, then remove from the heat. Continue to whisk until it has a nice, smooth consistency.

• Sprinkle with the chopped chives and you're good to go!

Blue cheese fondue

150g (5½oz) Young Buck cheese, rind removed and crumbled (Stilton would work, too)

150g (5½oz) Cornish Gouda cheese, rind removed and grated (any mature Gouda would also work)

8g (2 teaspoons) cornflour (cornstarch)

50ml (2fl oz) (hard) cider

50ml (2fl oz) double (heavy) cream

25ml (1fl oz) brandy

finely chopped chives, to garnish

This is a game changer of a fondue. We've learned from years of selling pots of fondue that people worry blue cheese might be a bit much to take on. Well, we're here to tell you that if you don't embrace this fondue, you're missing out on one of the most transcendental cheese experiences of your life.

• Place both cheeses in a bowl and mix together. Add the cornflour (cornstarch) and toss, ensuring the cheese is evenly coated.

• Pour the cider, cream and brandy into a fondue pot and bring to the boil.

• Reduce the heat and add the cheese mix.

• Whisk until the cheese has all melted and has a smooth consistency.

• Sprinkle with chopped chives and serve immediately.

Smoked fondue

225g (8oz) Smoked Lincolnshire Poacher cheese, rind removed and grated (Smoked Quicke's Cheddar or Smoked Westcombe Cheddar are also good)

75g (2¾oz) Ogleshield cheese, grated (or use raclette)

7g (¼oz) cornflour (cornstarch)

80ml (3fl oz) stout

2 teaspoons whisky

2 teaspoons lemon juice

1 teaspoon Worcestershire sauce

TO SERVE

20g (¾oz) smoked bacon, cooked until crispy

rosemary salt

Applewood Smoked Cheddar is the UK's best-selling smoked cheese, but is not actually smoked in the traditional sense. It's made with smoke flavour and paprika.

I'm not a big fan of Applewood. I prefer a smoked cheese – that has seen real smoke, has a good balance of flavour and where the smoke doesn't overpower the cheese. We came up with this smoked cheese fondue to celebrate those cheeses. It's made with stout in place of wine and a shot of whisky to give it a real punch.

- Place both cheeses in a bowl and mix together. Add the cornflour (cornstarch) and toss, ensuring the cheese is evenly coated.

- Pour the stout, whisky, lemon juice and Worcestershire sauce into a fondue pot and bring to the boil.

- Reduce the heat and add the cheese mix.

- Whisk until the cheese is just over half melted, then remove from the heat. Continue to whisk until you have a nice, smooth consistency.

- Garnish with crispy smoked bacon and rosemary salt to taste.

Moitié-moitié (half & half)

150g (5½oz) Mayfield cheese, rind removed and grated (Gruyére or Emmenthal would also work)

150g (5½oz) Yarlington cheese, cut into small cubes and rind left on (or another washed-rind cheese, such as Maida Vale or Limburger)

8g (2 teaspoons) cornflour (cornstarch)

1 garlic clove, halved

100ml (3½fl oz) white wine

25ml (1fl oz) kirsch (or brandy)

juice of ½ lemon

Moitié-moitié is a classic Swiss-style fondue, made with Gruyère and Vacherin Fribourgeois in equal half measures. Here we use Mayfield instead of Gruyère, which is a semi-hard Alpine-style cheese made in Sussex, and Yarlington instead of Vacherin, which is a soft washed-rind cheese made in Gloucestershire. We like the contrast they bring: you've got a sweet and innocent flavour from the Mayfield and then a healthy smack of funk from the Yarlington.

- Place both cheeses in a bowl and mix together. Add the cornflour (cornstarch) and toss, ensuring the cheese is evenly coated.

- Run the cut sides of the garlic clove halves around the base and sides of your fondue pot. Crush them and throw in the whole clove. Add the wine, kirsch and lemon juice to the pot and bring to the boil.

- Reduce the heat and add the cheese mix. Whisk until the cheese is just over half melted, then remove from the heat. Continue to whisk until you have a smooth consistency. Serve immediately.

Smoked mozzarella sticks with chilli honey

Makes 16–18 sticks

FOR THE MOZZARELLA STICKS

400–500g (14oz–1lb 2oz) whole smoked cooking mozzarella or smoked scamorza cheese (you want a single whole cheese that you can slice into batons.

90g (3¼oz) plain (all-purpose) flour

4 eggs, beaten

150g (5½oz) panko breadcrumbs

1 teaspoon dried oregano

1 teaspoon dried basil

1 teaspoon garlic powder

1 teaspoon table salt

½ teaspoon pepper

TO COOK AND SERVE

1–2 litres (2–4 pints) vegetable oil

140g (5oz) Chilli honey (see page 85)

80g (3oz) hard cheese (such as Spenwood, Berkswell or Parmesan), grated

If you need an incentive to make this recipe or fancy a laugh, then head to Google, type in "The Cheese Bar – Timeout" and check out the video tab. You'll find a video called: This is the cheesiest place in London!

The rather unflattering introduction to the video is me (Matthew), two days before opening a restaurant, tired and dishevelled with stringy mozzarella sticks hanging out of my mouth. Within 24 hours the video hit seven million views and we were left with endless queues.

To prepare the mozzarella sticks
• Cut the mozzarella into 20–25g (¾–1oz) batons; you should get 16–18 depending on the size of your whole cheese.

• Set up your coating (pané) station. You'll need two large bowls or dishes, and a smaller one. Place the flour in one of the large bowls, and the egg in the smaller one. In the other large bowl, mix together the panko, dried oregano, dried basil, garlic powder, salt and pepper.

• Set out your bowls in the following order: flour, egg, breadcrumbs. Lay out some nonstick baking (parchment) paper next to the breadcrumb bowl at the end. Now you're ready to pané!

• Take your first mozzarella stick. Coat it in flour, then transfer to the egg to coat, and then into the breadcrumb mix, ensuring you use one hand to just deal with the dry coating and the other for the wet to avoid the breadcrumb mixture clumping too quickly.

• Once evenly coated, place on the baking paper. Repeat with all the mozzarella sticks.

• When all the mozzarella has been panéed, you need to repeat with just the egg and breadcrumb stages.

To cook the mozzarella sticks
• In a large heavy-bottomed pan, heat the vegetable oil to 160°C (320°F); you can test the temperature with a sugar (candy) thermometer. If you don't have a thermometer, test the oil with a cube of bread. It should brown in 40–50 seconds when the oil is at the right temperature.

• Deep-fry the sticks in small batches, being careful not to overcrowd the pan. They will take 4–5 minutes each to cook; when you see mozzarella starting to leak out, they are ready to come out.

• Serve your mozzarella sticks hot, with the hard cheese grated over the top and the chilli honey for drizzling and dipping.

Chicken poutine

Serves 4

FOR THE ROASTED CHICKEN

½ yellow onion, roughly chopped

3 celery sticks, roughly chopped

2 carrots, roughly chopped

1 leek, roughly chopped

¼ bunch of thyme

¼ bunch of rosemary

¼ bunch of sage

1 whole chicken
(around 1.5kg/3lb 5oz)

50g (1¾oz) soft butter

FOR THE GRAVY

Makes 250–300ml (8½–10fl oz)

100ml (3½fl oz) white wine

1 heaped tablespoon plain
(all-purpose) flour

500ml (17fl oz) water

salt and pepper

FOR THE POUTINE

dash of olive oil

handful of sage (about 10 leaves)

320g (11½oz) cheese curds

750g (1lb 10oz) chips (fries)
(see page 55), hot

salt

Poutine is Canada's great cheese gift to the world. Essentially French fries covered with melted cheese curds and gravy, the dish first originated in Quebec, but today is served all over Canada.

We've come up with our own version that many Canadians would probably argue isn't proper poutine. But we think of it as poutine with a north London accent.

Making a good chicken gravy isn't a rush job. In our restaurant we simmer huge batches of stock for six hours to get a fully concentrated flavour. We've simplified things for the book, but you could make your own stock for a richer gravy by boiling the chicken bones in water with the vegetables for couple of hours. You can also buy chicken stock, and use it to replace the water in the gravy recipe.

Cheese curds are young, squeaky curds from the very early stages of cheesemaking, such as Cheddar. They are not curd cheese, which is soft, fresh and spreadable. And grated cheese is not the same either.

Cheese curds are not widely available in the UK, but you can find them in delis and farm shops, or buy online from cheesemakers, including Westcombe Dairy or Batch Farm in Somerset.

To roast the chicken
- Preheat the oven to 200°C (400°F), Gas Mark 6.

- Put the vegetables and herbs in a baking tray and lay the chicken on top. Smear the butter on the skin, especially the breasts and legs.

- Roast in the oven for 30 minutes. Then turn the heat down to 180°C (350°F), Gas Mark 4 and roast for another 40 minutes. Remove from the oven and check the chicken is cooked, either by piercing one of the legs with a skewer and checking the juices run clear or by using a digital meat thermometer to ensure it has reached 70°C (160°F). Leave the oven on for the chips (fries).

- Remove the chicken from the pan to rest and, once cool, peel off the skin and shred the meat, reserving the skin for later.

To make the gravy
- Put the roasting pan on the hob with the vegetables still in it, and deglaze with the white wine, scraping the bottom with a spoon so that all the juices and sticky residue from the chicken are dissolved. Then stir in the flour and slowly add the water and any resting juices.

Recipe continues overleaf

- Allow to reduce until the desired consistency then remove from the heat and pass through a sieve.

Finally, it's glory time, compile the poutine
- Cook the chips according to the recipe on page 55.

- Lay the reserved chicken skin on a tray and put in the oven with the chips for 8-10 minutes until crisp. Season with salt.

- Coat the bottom of a frying pan over a medium-high heat with the oil and heat until shimmering, then add the sage leaves, spreading them out so they are in a single layer.

- Fry for around 30 seconds until they are crisp. Remove and place on kitchen paper (paper towels) to drain.

- Next, add the gravy to a small saucepan and bring to a simmer. When it starts to simmer, add the shredded chicken and let it cook for another 2 minutes until the chicken is piping hot.

- Spread the fresh curds over the top of the hot chips and pour over the chicken and gravy. The gravy will melt the cheese.

- Top with the crispy sage and chicken skin and tuck straight in!

SONG PAIRING • SONG PAIRING • SONG PAIRING • SONG PAIRING •

Heart of Gold
NEIL YOUNG

A meeting of two of Canada's finest exports. It will melt your heart.

Blue cheese & pastrami raclette

Serves 4

FOR THE CRISPY LEEKS

1 leek

1 egg

flour, for coating

150ml (5fl oz) vegetable oil

FOR THE RACLETTE

250g (9oz) leeks

olive oil, for frying

500g (1lb 2oz) baby new
potatoes

250g (9oz) thick-cut pastrami
(not overly peppered), sliced

½ bunch of chives, finely chopped

½ bunch of chervil, finely
chopped

480g (1lb 1oz) Young Buck
(or another punchy blue, sliced
into 120g (4¼oz) triangles (see
page 192 on how to cut cheese)

60ml (4 tablespoons) truffle
honey (you can use plain honey,
if you prefer)

salt and pepper

An umami bomb of a dish that has been on the menu for many years.
We use salt beef, which we simmer in spices and herbs for eight
hours until it is falling apart, but pastrami also works well with creamy,
spicy blue cheese. Just make sure to buy a thick-cut pastrami that
isn't overly coated in pepper.

For the cheese, we use Young Buck – a raw milk blue from Northern
Ireland, but Stilton would work just as well. You want a punchy blue
that will bring plenty of savoury sizzle.

One last thing: we've called this dish blue cheese raclette from
the very beginning, but you could argue that the way it is made
has more in common with tartiflette. Either way it has the same
ending: deliciousness!

To make the crispy leeks
- Remove the green leaves and the outer layer of the leek and
  wash thoroughly. Cut in half lengthways and try to keep the halves
  intact. Dry thoroughly then slice each half into thin, French
  fry-shaped batons.

- Whisk the egg in small bowl and dust some flour on a plate.

- Heat the oil in large, heavy-bottomed pan to 160°C (320°F) on
  a sugar (candy) thermometer. If you don't have a thermometer,
  test the oil with a cube of bread. It should brown in 40-50 seconds
  when the oil is at the right temperature.

- Working in small batches, dip the leek fries in egg, then in the flour and
  then shake off any excess before dropping them in the hot oil. Deep-
  fry the leeks in batches for 2–3 minutes until they turn golden brown.

- Carefully remove from the oil and allow to drain on kitchen paper
  (paper towels), then set aside.

To make the raclette
- Preheat the oven to 200°C (400°F), Gas Mark 6.

- Remove the green leaves and the outer layer of the leeks. Wash them
  thoroughly, then slice on the diagonal into thin rings.

- Heat a frying pan over a high heat and add a small amount of oil.
  Fry the leeks for around 8-10 minutes until they are soft with a nice
  charring to them.

Recipe continues overleaf

- While the leeks are cooking, place the potatoes in a pan of salted water and bring to the boil. Boil for 10–15 minutes until a fork easily slips into them.

- When the leeks and potatoes are cooked, mix with the pastrami, chives and chervil and season with salt and pepper.

- Split the mix between 4 skillets or ovenproof dishes. (You could also make one sharing portion in a large ovenproof dish.)

- Pour 1 tablespoon of water over the potato mix in each skillet and top each one with a 120g (4¼oz) layer of blue cheese.

- Put the skillets or dishes in the oven for 15 minutes until the cheese is melted and the dish is piping hot. If you're making one large dish for sharing, cook in the oven for 20–25 minutes.

- To serve, top with a drizzle of truffle honey and a handful of crispy leeks.

SINGING THE BLUES

Christmas isn't Christmas without Stilton. In fact, Brits eat so much Stilton during the festive season that November and December account for almost half the annual sales of some producers.

The crumbly cows' milk cheese is protected by law with a Protected Designation of Origin (PDO), meaning it can only be made in Leicestershire, Derbyshire and Nottinghamshire. The tight controls mean there are only six Stilton makers left in the country. The two best for our money are Colston Bassett and Cropwell Bishop.

But blue cheese is for life, not just for Christmas, and there's plenty to choose from. France is famous for Roquefort, a raw sheep's milk blue that is soft and salty and spicy. In Lombardy, Italy, Gorgonzola is made in two different styles: dolce, which is so soft and sweet it can be scooped like ice cream; and piccante, a crumblier version that has plenty of peppery bite.

There's been a boom in new blues in recent years, too. Stilton-style cheeses such as Young Buck and Stichelton each have their own distinct personalities, while there are softer, more European styles, such as Cote Hill Blue, Pevensey Blue and Beauvale. Plus different milk types, from Beenleigh Blue and Lanark Blue (both made with sheep's milk), to Harbourne and Biggar Blue (goats' milk). Shepherd's Purse in Yorkshire makes an uber-creamy Buffalo Blue, made with milk from a British herd of water buffaloes.

What all these cheeses have in common is a vibrant mould, called *Penicillium roqueforti*, which grows inside the cheese, creating beautiful veins, streaks and patches of blue and green. The mould is added to the milk during cheesemaking and lies dormant in the cheese until it is pierced with sharp metal skewers during maturation. At this point oxygen flows into the cheese, breathing life into the moulds, which then slowly spread through the body, softening the texture and bringing wonderful boozy, peppery and tangy flavours.

How people first discovered that mouldy blue cheese tasted delicious is lost to history. There's an apocryphal tale that Roquefort was invented a thousand years ago when an amorous young shepherd was distracted by a beautiful woman and left his lunch of rye bread and white sheep's cheese in one of the region's famous caves. He returned several days later to find the bread had turned mouldy and caused the curd to develop blue veins. Despite appearances, he bravely gave the blue cheese a nibble and found it to be delectable.

There's another fun story behind the reason Stilton is so associated with Christmas. The theory goes that the best cheeses are made in September with creamy end-of-summer milk. Stilton needs three months to mature, which means the cheeses are ready just in time for the festive period. Pass the port!

Hebridean Blue stuffed prunes

Makes 5

10 large dried prunes

50g (1¾oz) Hebridean Blue or Roquefort, cut into 5 rectangular pieces

3 smoked streaky (lean) bacon rashers, halved widthways

1 teaspoon olive oil

Could there be a more perfect bar snack than these salty, sweet nuggets? Plump prunes, wrapped in bacon and stuffed with a feisty Scottish blue from the Isle of Mull. I mean, come on.

If you can't get Hebridean Blue, Roquefort or any spicy blue would work just fine.

Be warned: this recipe makes five prunes, but five is never enough. Consider doubling or tripling!

- Preheat the oven to 200°C (400°F), Gas Mark 6. Line an oven tray with nonstick baking (parchment) paper.

- Slice the prunes halfway through lengthways (don't fully separate the two halves), and remove any seeds.

- Sandwich each portion of cheese between 2 prunes. Lay out the bacon slices and securely wrap around the prunes and cheese (think pigs-in-blanket-style). You want the bacon to go around the prune a maximum of 1.5 times.

- Heat the olive oil in a frying pan over a medium-high heat. Cook the bacon-wrapped prunes for 3 minutes, rotating as they cook to evenly colour the bacon all the way around.

- Place the prunes on the lined tray and cook in the oven for 3–5 minutes or until the cheese starts to ooze out. Be careful not to leave them too long, as you don't want all the cheese to escape. Serve hot from the oven.

SONG PAIRING · SONG PAIRING · SONG PAIRING · SONG PAIRING ·

I Had Too Much To Dream
THE ELECTRIC PRUNES

Expect wild dreams if you eat these before bedtime.

Jalapeño poppers with garlic & herb dip

Makes 14–16 poppers

FOR THE JALAPEÑO POPPERS

150g (5½oz) pickled jalapeños
(drained weight)

125g (4½oz) mascarpone cheese

275g (9¾oz) cooking mozzarella
or scamorza cheese, grated

100g (3½oz) plain (all-purpose)
flour

5 eggs, beaten

250g (9oz) panko breadcrumbs

1 litre (2 pints) vegetable oil,
for deep-frying

salt and pepper

FOR THE GARLIC AND HERB DIP

1 clove of confit garlic
(see page 87)

175ml (6fl oz) soured cream

1 tablespoon mayonnaise

½ teaspoon dried thyme

½ teaspoon dried oregano

salt

These chilli and cheese bombs are guaranteed to make you hot under the collar. Beneath their crispy, golden exterior lies an explosion of spicy chillies and velvety mozzarella.

They pair perfectly with a margarita, or even a dirty margarita (see additional recipe below). Hot Stuff by Donna Summer must be played at the same time. It's the law!

To make the jalapeño poppers

- Add the drained jalapeños to a blender or food processor and blitz them until finely chopped. In small batches, place the blitzed jalapeños in kitchen paper (paper towels) and squeeze to dry.

- In a bowl, mix the mascarpone and chillies together and season before finally adding the grated mozzarella. Shape the mix into ovals (about 30g/1oz each) and pané them (see page 70) by rolling in the flour, then the egg and then the breadcrumbs.

- In a large heavy-bottomed pan, heat the vegetable oil to 160°C (320°F); you can test the temperature with a sugar (candy) thermometer. If you don't have a thermometer, test the oil with a cube of bread. It should brown in 40–50 seconds when the oil is at the right temperature.

- Deep-fry the poppers in batches of 3 or 4 for 3–5 minutes until golden brown and piping hot.

To make the garlic and herb dip

- Mash the confit garlic with the back of a fork to make a rough purée.

- In a bowl, mix together the remaining ingredients. Add the confit garlic purée and gently mix. Taste and add table salt if required.

Dirty Margarita

lime wedge

table salt, for dipping

1 tablespoon lime juice

3 slices (rings) of pickled
jalapeños

30ml (5 teaspoons) Tequila or
Mezcal

20ml (4 teaspoons) Cointreau

1 tablespoon agave syrup

1 teaspoon pickled jalapeño liquor

ice

- Wipe the rim of a rocks glass with the lime wedge and dip into salt to coat the rim.

- Place the lime juice and 2 of the jalapeño rings in a shaker and muddle.

- Add the Tequila, Cointreau, lime juice, agave syrup, pickle liquor and ice, then shake well.

- Fill the glass with fresh ice, the pour over the margarita through a strainer and garnish with the remaining jalapeño ring and lime wedge.

Curried Cheddar curds

Serves 2

FOR THE CHILLI HONEY

Makes 250g (9oz)

(Side note: this goes with ABSOLUTELY EVERYTHING.)

250g (9oz) honey

½ fresh red chilli, roughly chopped

pinch of table salt

FOR THE CURDS

Makes 6 portions

160ml (5½fl oz) whole milk

325g (11½oz) semolina flour

500g (1lb 2oz) cheese curds (see page 73 – we use Westcombe Cheddar curds)

FOR THE DISH

1 litre (2 pints) vegetable oil, for deep-frying

150g (5½oz) coated curds

10g (¼oz) mild curry powder

pinch of sea salt flakes

30g (1oz) chilli honey (see above)

This dish is one of the big hitters on The Cheese Barge, a must-order if you pay us a visit. We hate to blow our own trumpet, but restaurant critic Grace Dent did refer to them as one of the best things she ate in 2021...

Curds are the first stage of cheesemaking – they are fresh, salty and deceptively moreish. They are adored in the US and Canada, served with poutine (see page 73), fried on their own or eaten fresh from the bag.

So, what makes this dish so good? Simplicity! Squeaky curds, fried in a light batter, then tossed in curry powder and chilli honey. Salty, sweet and delicious with a little bit of heat. God tier snacking!

To make the chilli honey
- Pour the honey into a small saucepan and add the chilli and salt.

- Place the pan over a low heat and gently warm up the honey for 5 minutes. You don't want it to boil but just be heated through. Remove from the heat and allow to cool.

- Once cooled, strain the mixture through a colander to remove the chilli pieces.

- Taste the chilli honey. If it's too spicy for your liking, then you can add some more honey to dilute it down. This can be made in advance and stored in an airtight container in a cool, dry place for up to 1 month.

To prepare the curds
- Set yourself up with two bowls. Add the milk to one, and the semolina to the other.

- Add the curds to the bowl of milk and give them a good mix.

- Once mixed, lift them out and drop them into the semolina flour and mix to cover them. Aim to get a consistent coverage of flour. Lift the curds out of the flour and shake off any excess.

- Repeat the process again with the semolina-coated curds, dropping them into the milk, then the semolina again and finally shake, shake, shake to get the excess off.

- These are now ready to fry. They will keep in a tub in the refrigerator until you're ready to fry them. They'll stay good for up to 5 days.

Recipe continues overleaf

DRINKS PAIRING · DRINKS PAIRING · DRINKS PAIRING · DRINKS PAIRING ·

Pilsner lager

Cold, crisp and refreshing, Pilsner makes the spice sing.

To serve

- In a large heavy-bottomed pan, heat the vegetable oil to 180°C (356°F) using a sugar (candy) thermometer. If you don't have a thermometer, test the oil with a cube of bread. It should brown in 30-40 seconds when the oil is at the right temperature.

- Carefully drop the coated curds into the hot oil. Deep-fry for about 2-3 minutes until golden brown and crispy.

- Remove from the oil and allow to drain on kitchen paper (paper towels) to remove excess oil.

- Now to add some flavour! Place the cooked curds in a bowl and generously dust with mild curry powder and a pinch of sea salt, shaking well to get a good coverage.

- Serve the curds in a bowl with a good helping of chilli honey over the top.

Lancashire aligot & Cumberland sausage

Serves 4

FOR THE CONFIT GARLIC BUTTER

Makes 315g (11oz)

125ml (4fl oz) olive oil

65g (2¼oz) garlic, peeled

250g (9oz) salted butter, at room temperature

FOR THE STICKY ONIONS

2 tablespoons olive oil

1 red onion, sliced

1 yellow onion, sliced

1 garlic clove, finely chopped

75ml (2½fl oz) red wine

2 teaspoons balsamic vinegar

1½ tablespoons caster (superfine) sugar

1 teaspoon mixed dried herbs

salt and pepper

FOR THE ALIGOT

250g (9oz) potatoes (King Edward/Maris Piper/Russet), skin on, cut into 4cm (1½-inch) chunks

60g (2¼oz) confit garlic butter (see above)

60ml (4 tablespoons) full-fat (whole) milk

150g (5½oz) Kirkham's Lancashire cheese, grated (or other crumbly cheeses, see note)

100g (3½oz) cooking mozzarella or unsmoked scamorza cheese

salt and pepper

TO SERVE

8 Cumberland sausages

One of the world's greatest cheese dishes, aligot hails from the L'Aubrac region in the South of France where it's traditionally made with Tomme de Laguiole or other Tomme-style cheeses.

Tommes are semi-hard cheeses that are made in the mountains across Europe. They're buttery and earthy, and melt beautifully.

It's a simple dish of cheese, potatoes and garlic normally served with a good Toulouse sausage. But we've given it a British twist by using crumbly Kirkham's Lancashire and a Cumberland sausage instead.

To make the confit garlic butter
- Put the oil and garlic in a pan over a low heat. Cook slowly for 10 minutes until the garlic is soft. Drain off the oil and leave to cool.

- Crush the confit garlic with the back of a fork until it has broken down into a paste. Add to a bowl with the butter and whip until smooth. You'll need 60g (2¼oz) of this for the dish – the rest will keep in an airtight container in the refrigerator for 2 weeks, or in the freezer for 1 month.

To make the sticky onions
- Heat the olive oil in a frying pan over a gentle heat and cook the onions for 10 minutes until soft.

- Add to a stock pot with all the remaining ingredients and cook, over a medium heat, until the liquid has reduced to a thick, sticky consistency, about 5–10 minutes. Remove from the heat and set aside.

To make the aligot
- Place the potatoes in a pan of salted water and bring to the boil. Boil until tender (15–20 minutes), then drain and peel the skins using a tea towel to rub them away.

- Mash the potatoes until they're as smooth as possible. It's best to put them through a potato ricer or mouli and then push them through a sieve to purée them for the silkiest results.

- Cook the sausages in a frying pan over a medium heat for 8–12 minutes. Make sure to turn during cooking, until piping hot and cooked through.

- When the sausages are cooked, set aside in a warm place, pour away the fat from the pan and then add the sticky onions with a splash of water. Place over a low heat to gently reheat.

Recipe continues overleaf

- While you are cooking the sausages and onions, you can continue making the aligot. Place the mashed potatoes in a pan with the confit garlic butter, and half the milk. Mix and then place over a medium–high heat for a few minutes until hot.

- Reduce the heat to medium and then stir the grated Lancashire into the potato mix with a wooden spoon until it melts. When you first add the cheese, it'll look lumpy, but as the mash gets hotter, the cheese will melt, until you reach a smooth consistency. The mix should be reasonably thick but dropping off the spoon. If it's too thick, add a splash more of the milk.

- Add the grated mozzarella to the mash and forcefully beat, still over a medium heat. Keep beating it relentlessly until the mash becomes stringy and pulls away from the side of the pan.

- Season the mash with salt and pepper, and serve immediately in a warm dish. Place the mash in first, sausages on top and then spoon over the sticky onions. Dig in straight away while it's hot and stringy.

Note: Other crumbly cheeses, such as Wensleydale, also work in place of Kirkham's Lancashire. Or try a French Tomme (rind removed).

Alpines and grana cheeses

Size matters, especially when it comes to a family of *fromages* known as the Alpines. These large, hard cheeses are inextricably linked to mountains, particularly the Alps, and include everything from Gruyère and Emmenthal in Switzerland and bergkäse in Germany, to Comté and Beaufort in France.

Made as a way of storing the glut of summer milk, which comes when cows graze mountain pastures in bloom with wild grasses, flowers and herbs, these cheeses are big and low in moisture so they can be aged for a long time. Certainly long enough to last the snowy winters that restrict movement in the mountains.

Each has a unique character. Emmenthal, the biggest, is made in enormous, holey wheels weighing over 100kg (220lb), with a pliable texture and yeasty flavour. Its sister cheese Gruyère, pressed in 35kg (77lb) discs, is more powerful, with tropical fruit and roast beef notes. Comté, on the other hand, often has caramel and hazelnut notes.

In Italy, they make equally big cheeses, but in a slightly different way. Parmigiano Reggiano and Grana Padano, known as 'grana' (grainy) cheeses, come in 40kg (88lb) drums and are aged for years until they are hard and crystalline with wonderful roasted pineapple flavours.

They are styles of cheese that British makers have struggled to replicate. That's partly because the terroir is different. Ben Nevis is a lot smaller and wetter than the Alps. But also because it takes a lot of investment to make huge cheeses that sit in maturing rooms for years before you get paid.

A few British cheeses have the fruity flavour that makes Alpine and grana cheeses so popular, however. Lincolnshire Poacher, a kind of Cheddar-Gruyère hybrid, and Cornish Kern, which is part Gouda, part Comté, are both good Alpine alternatives. Old Winchester is a good option instead of Parmesan.

Malakoffs

Makes 6

* You will need an 8–9cm (3–3½-inch) pastry cutter (cookie cutter) or something of that diameter to cut around

65g (2¼oz) plain (all-purpose) flour

½ teaspoon table salt

pinch of black pepper

½ teaspoon finely grated nutmeg

400g (14oz) strong hard cheese, finely grated (Gruyère is traditional, but Doddington or Cheddar work too)

2 large (US extra-large) eggs

1 garlic clove, finely grated

25g (1oz) Marmite

50ml (2fl oz) white wine

6 slices medium-sliced bread (generic white sliced works best)

1–2 litres (2–4 pints) vegetable oil, for deep-frying

cornichons, to garnish (optional)

green salad, to serve

Malakoffs are a kind of fondue fritter from Switzerland. Deep-fried with a gooey centre, traditionally they would be made with Gruyère and white wine. However, ours feature Doddington, a sort of Cheddar-Parmesan hybrid cheese from Northumberland, and Marmite. You either love it or you hate it, right?

Make sure you've got the perfect golden crunch and oozing cheese spilling out when you cut into it.

· In a large bowl, mix the flour, salt, pepper and nutmeg. Mix in the cheese, evenly coating with the flour mixture.

· In a separate bowl, whisk together the eggs, garlic, Marmite and wine.

· Add this to the cheese mixture and mix well to form a thick paste.

· Using an 8–9cm (3–3½-inch) circular pastry cutter (cookie cutter), cut 6 discs out of the bread. Save the crusts for breadcrumbs.

· Take one sixth of the cheese mix and shape into a dome on top of a bread disc. You're aiming for the dome to be about 2cm (¾-inch) high in the middle and for the sides of the bread to also be covered. Repeat until you have six Malakoffs.

· Heat the oil in a large heavy-bottomed pan to 160°C (320°F). Check using a sugar (candy) thermometer. If you don't have a thermometer, test the oil with a cube of bread. It should brown in 40–50 seconds when the oil is at the right temperature.

· Carefully drop the Malakoffs into the oil cheese-side down and cook for 2–3 minutes. When the domes look golden brown, flip them over to cook the bread for 1 minute.

· Carefully remove from the oil and allow to drain on kitchen paper (paper towels).

· Serve hot with some cornichons and a green salad.

Jazz Reeves

Affineur

Paxton & Whitfield

Paxton & Whitfield has been selling cheese for over 200 years, making it the oldest cheesemonger in Britain and quite possibly the world. It's best known for its flagship shop in Piccadilly, London, but is actually headquartered in the Cotswolds where it has state-of-the-art maturing rooms, used to age cheese to perfection – a process called affinage.

Jazz Reeves is in charge of these temperature- and humidity-controlled rooms in her job as an affineur (cheese maturer), tending the cheeses on a daily basis to make sure they ripen to their full potential. "They're living, breathing products that need a lot of care," she explains. "It's how I imagine raising children must be like. Small things add up to big differences over time."

These "small things" include monitoring and adjusting the temperature and humidity, brushing and turning the cheeses, patting down moulds and washing some in brine.

"It's a perfect balance between creativity and science. We're always asking, 'What can we do to make this cheese better?'"

Sampling long-ageing cheeses, such as Cheddar and Comté, is also a big part of the job. This is done using a tool called a cheese iron (cheese trier) to extract a core of cheese that can be pressed, sniffed and tasted.

"I love the fact that each batch is different to the next," says Jazz. "We have to assess what we think a cheese might taste like many months down the line. If you pick delicate savoury and brothy notes in a Cheddar at six months, it's probably going to be even more intense and delicious at 18 months. But if it's already got a punchy flavour, in another year it could get quite gnarly and unbalanced."

Originally from Manchester, Jazz started in cheese in 2015 when she moved to Stratford-upon-Avon after finishing her music degree (she still plays drums in a band). A job advert in the window of Paxton & Whitfield's shop caught her eye and she took a chance and applied. After working as a cheesemonger and reading every book she could find on affinage, she ended up becoming queen of the maturing rooms in 2020.

"I feel like I'm a custodian of the cheese," she says. "If you think how much effort goes into rearing animals, milking them and making cheese, it's a privilege to be the next step in the process."

Estelle Reynolds

Cheesemonger

Neal's Yard Dairy, London

Like many people, Estelle Reynolds discovered the joy of cheese through a good cheese shop.

Neal's Yard Dairy has been a pioneer of British cheese for more than 40 years and its shop in Borough Market is a destination for cheese lovers from all over the world. Estelle, who previously worked in pub and bar management, had long admired its approach.

"I was always taken with the vibe and atmosphere at Neal's Yard Dairy, so I applied for a job as a Christmas temp in 2010," she explains. "It was really full on, but I enjoyed the hustle and bustle and seeing how happy people were with their Christmas cheese. I also loved tasting cheese in the shop with customers and seeing how engaged they were."

She enjoyed it so much that she never left and now oversees all of Neal's Yard Dairy's shops in the capital. She still works some days behind the counter at Borough, but also switches between the other shops in Covent Garden, Islington and Bermondsey, as well as visiting farms and cheesemakers.

A typical day starts with setting up the impressive display of cheeses, trimming them as she goes so they are in perfect condition and making sure they are tightly wrapped so they don't dry out.

"I love being so hands on with food," she says. "We see and feel the cheeses every day and can really notice the seasonal changes. We sell a lot of raw milk, farmhouse cheeses that have a lot of variation. It's exciting to see those changes and share them with the customers."

The display is deconstructed at the end of every day and the shop thoroughly scrubbed down. "You spend a lot of time cleaning as a cheesemonger," she says. The other big preoccupation is staying warm in the cool cheese room during winter. Estelle can reel off the names of all the best brands for thermal layers and insoles. "We always give new staff the talk about the best gear. You need layers that are thin so you can move easily, but super warm at the same time."

This camaraderie is something Estelle loves about being a cheesemonger. "You meet really interesting people, who are part-time cheesemongers, but also working as a musician, actor or in fashion and design. We're all from the city and have different backgrounds, but we're all really interested in the countryside and where our food comes from."

Ba

ke

Cheese puffs with Gouda cream

FOR THE PUFFS

Makes 25

115g (4oz) water

115g (4oz) full-fat (whole) milk

90g (3¼oz) butter

145g (5¼oz) plain (all-purpose) flour

4 large (US extra-large) eggs, beaten, plus 1 extra to glaze

180g (6½oz) Gouda cheese, grated

pinch of ground nutmeg

salt and pepper

FOR THE GOUDA CREAM

100g (3½oz) Gouda cheese, grated

½ teaspoon cornflour (cornstarch)

200ml (7fl oz) double (heavy) cream

salt and pepper

In France they're known as "gougères", but we like to call them cheese puffs! Either way they are made with choux pastry, enriched with cheese and baked until light and airy with a crisp, golden shell. They sound complicated but are actually fairly simple to make. The only problem is that it's hard not to scoff them all in one sitting.

Top tip: Have some of these ready in the freezer, to whip out and bake at any moment. They bake even better from frozen than they do from fresh. Simply pipe them onto baking trays, put cling film (plastic wrap) over the top and place them in the freezer till solid. Then consolidate into airtight boxes. When you want to eat, bake from frozen in the oven at 200°C (400°F), Gas Mark 6 for 25–30 minutes.

To make the puffs
• Preheat the oven to 200°C (400°F), Gas Mark 6. Line a few baking trays with nonstick baking (parchment) paper.

• In a medium saucepan, combine the measured water, milk and butter and bring to a gentle simmer.

• While still over the heat, add the flour and salt and pepper. Stir and cook until you get a smooth, uniform dough: it should be pulling away from the sides of the pan. This should take about 2–3 minutes.

• Remove from the heat and beat in the eggs, adding them a little at a time and waiting until each addition is fully incorporated before adding more.

• Allow the dough to cool, then add three-quarters of the Gouda and the nutmeg.

Recipe continues overleaf

SONG PAIRING • SONG PAIRING • SONG PAIRING • SONG PAIRING •

Take Me I'm Yours
MARY CLARK

You know when it gets down to that last cheese puff, this song is sending you a message...

- Transfer to piping (pastry) bags, then pipe puffs onto the lined baking trays. Each puff should be about the size of a walnut and spaced well apart as they will expand. With the final beaten egg, brush a glaze on the top of each puff and then sprinkle each with all the remaining Gouda.

- Place the trays in the oven and cook for 22–25 minutes until golden brown. Remove from the oven and use a skewer to poke a hole in each puff to release the steam.

To make the Gouda cream
- In a bowl, toss the grated Gouda in the cornflour (cornstarch).

- Heat the cream in a saucepan. When the cream starts to boil, reduce the heat and add the cheese. Whisk until fully melted, then season with salt and pepper.

- Eat immediately, dipping the puffs in the Gouda cream.

Feta & tomato filo tart

Makes a 23cm (9-inch) tart, serves 4

* You will need a 23cm (9-inch) tart tin

FOR THE FILLING

160g (5¾oz) feta cheese (or Graceburn, see recipe introduction)

115g (4oz) cream cheese

30g (1oz) semolina

2 tablespoons milk

2 eggs, beaten

zest of 1 lemon

½ teaspoon black pepper

FOR THE BASIL OIL

25g (1oz) picked basil leaves (½ bunch)

75ml (2½fl oz) olive oil

FOR THE TART

270g (9½oz) (1 packet) filo (phyllo) pastry sheets – 7 sheets

50g (1¾oz) butter, melted

300g (10½oz) baby tomatoes, halved or quartered

70g (2½oz) feta cheese (or Graceburn, drained and crumbled, see introduction)

lemon balm or finely chopped mint leaves, to garnish

This tart is perfect for a hot summer evening with a cheeky bottle of rosé. You can make it in advance and serve it cold, so there's no missing out on the golden hour.

Try to get 100 per cent sheep's milk feta if possible – it's sweeter and creamier than the cheeses with added goats' milk. We use a cheese called Graceburn for this dish in the restaurants. Made in Kent by Blackwoods Cheese Company, it looks a little like feta, but is made with raw cows' milk and is kept in jars filled with golden rapeseed (canola) oil with thyme, garlic and black pepper, which add a wonderful rich, herbaceous flavour.

- Preheat the oven to 180°C (350°F), Gas Mark 4.

- In a bowl, add all the ingredients for the filling and beat together until you have a smooth, consistent texture.

- Using a blender, blitz together the ingredients for the basil oil then strain through a muslin cloth or tea towel.

- To assemble the tarts, cut each pastry sheet in half to create 14 sheets. Each should measure roughly 25cm (9¾-inches) square.

- Brush the tin with some of the melted butter, before adding one half sheet of pastry. Butter the pastry and then add another half sheet with the corners at a different angle to the first sheet. Repeat for the rest of the sheets, continually turning to a different angle and fanning out the sheets slightly so they cover the sides of the tin.

- Spoon the filling mixture into the tart tin, before topping with the tomatoes and crumbled feta. Leave the overhanging pastry.

- Bake the tart for 20–25 minutes until the pastry is golden and crisp.

- Drizzle over the basil oil and sprinkle lemon balm or mint leaves on top of the tart.

Stichelton & beef bourguignon pie

Serves 4-6

* You will need a round ovenproof dish around 20-23cm (8-9 inches)

FOR THE FILLING

800g (1lb 12oz) beef shin (shank) or chuck, diced

2 tablespoons vegetable oil

100g (3½oz) bacon lardons

50g (1¾oz) silverskin (pearl) onions

50g (1¾oz) button (white) mushrooms

½ Spanish onion, peeled and chopped into 2cm (¾-inch) dice

1 leek, chopped into 2cm (¾-inch) dice

1 garlic clove, roughly chopped

1 carrot, peeled and chopped into 2cm (¾-inch) dice

1 stick of celery, chopped into 2cm (¾-inch) dice

20g (¾oz) tomato purée (paste)

250ml (8½fl oz) red wine

350ml (12fl oz) water

2 beef stock cubes

¼ bunch of rosemary

¼ bunch of thyme

1 bay leaf

salt and pepper

FOR THE PIE

200g (7oz) Stichelton cheese (or Stilton)

1 egg, beaten

500g (1lb 2oz) pre-rolled shortcrust pastry (pie dough), cut into a lid slightly larger than the ovenproof dish

What could be more comforting than slow-cooked beef bourguignon? How about beef bourguignon topped with pastry and blue cheese! Sara Lewis, head chef at The Cheese Barge, came up with this incredible pie one winter and we can't get enough of it.

We use Stichelton, a raw milk blue made in Nottinghamshire. It's made in a similar way to Stilton, but can't be called as such because Stilton is a protected cheese, and must be made with pasteurized milk by law. It's sweet, tangy, meaty and biscuity (cracker-like) all at once.

• Preheat the oven to 180°C (350°F), Gas Mark 4. Season the beef with salt and pepper. Heat the oil in a large frying pan and brown the meat in batches over a high heat for 5-10 minutes.

• Remove the beef from the pan and set aside. Add the bacon lardons to the same pan and cook over low heat until well rendered, about 5 minutes. Remove from the pan and set aside. Add the silverskin (pearl) onions to the pan and cook in the remaining fat until caramelized, about 5-10 minutes. Remove from pan and drain off any excess fat.

• Add all the vegetables and sweat over a low heat in the same pan until caramelized, about 10 minutes. Add the tomato purée (paste) and red wine, then add the measured water and stock cubes. Bring to the boil.

• Tightly wrap the herbs together with string. Transfer the beef, onions, and vegetable and stock mixture into an ovenproof dish and mix well. Add the herbs. Lay nonstick baking (parchment) paper over the top and cover with foil. Place in the oven and cook for 5 hours until the meat is tender.

• Ladle out all the liquid into a pan and simmer over a high heat, until reduced by half to get a thick saucy consistency.

• Increase the temperature of the oven to 200°C (400°F), Gas Mark 6.

• Return the braising liquid to the meat and veg in the ovenproof dish. Crumble two thirds of the cheese across the top. Slice the remaining third into very thin slices.

• Brush a little beaten egg around the rim of your dish and cover with the shortcrust pastry (pie dough), pushing it in around the edges of the dish. Cut a cross in the middle. Glaze the pastry with the remaining egg.

• Bake for 30 minutes until the pastry is golden. Remove from the oven and immediately lay the slices of cheese on top of the hot pastry. Serve with a leafy salad and a large glass of red wine!

Baked feta & stewed peppers

Serves 4 as a starter

FOR THE DRESSING

1 red chilli, deseeded

2 garlic cloves, peeled

juice of 1 lemon

1 teaspoon honey

salt

FOR THE DISH

2 red (bell) peppers

1 tablespoon oil (preferably from your feta)

250g (9oz) tomatoes, thinly sliced and deseeded (keep the seeds aside for later)

25g (1oz) caramelized onions (see page 52)

1 teaspoon smoked paprika

200g (7oz) feta or Graceburn cheese, drained from oil

salt and pepper

crusty bread, to serve

Salty and tangy, feta holds its shape beautifully when baked, becoming soft and fluffy rather than fully melting. Its flavours naturally work with other Mediterranean ingredients – red (bell) peppers, tomatoes and honey – in this delicious dish for dipping.

In our restaurants we use a British alternative called Graceburn. Softer than feta, it develops a lovely marshmallow puff texture on top of the tomato and pepper stew. See page 106 for more on feta.

To make the dressing

- Place the chilli and garlic in a blender or food processor with the lemon juice.

- Blitz until the contents have been cut to chunks; this might take a bit of time. Halfway through, add the honey and blitz until you have tiny chunks and a runny consistency.

- Pour into a bowl and season with salt to taste.

- The final taste should be spicy, sweet and slightly acidic from the lemon. You should be able to taste everything, including the salt.

To make the dish

- Preheat the oven to 200°C (400°F), Gas Mark 6.

- Start by giving the (bell) peppers a good char all over on the gas flame on the hob (stove). Use barbecue tongs or a fork to hold each pepper over a high heat, so you don't burn your fingers. You're looking to get a blackened skin all over.

- Once charred, wait for the peppers to cool a little and then carefully remove the skins and deseed them, then cut them into thin slices and set aside.

Recipe continues overleaf

DRINKS PAIRING · DRINKS PAIRING · DRINKS PAIRING · DRINKS PAIRING ·

Xinomavro

A marvellous Mediterranean match. Xinomavro is Greece's answer to Nebbiolo, used to make juicy, earthy red wines.

- Place the oil, tomato seeds and caramelized onions in a skillet or oven dish over a low heat. Start to sauté, and then add water to just cover the onions. Turn the heat to high until all the water evaporates. Re-cover with water and cook until it evaporates again. Repeat four or five times until the onion becomes almost a purée.

- Add the reserved peeled and sliced peppers, tomatoes and smoked paprika to the pan over a high heat. Cook for 3–4 minutes until it has reduced and become a nice saucy consistency. You may need to add a few tablespoons of water.

- Add large chunks of feta on top and place in the oven for 15-20 minutes, until the cheese becomes soft, fluffy and slightly golden.

- Finish with a healthy drizzle of the dressing and a good grind of black pepper over the feta. Serve with crusty bread for dipping. It also makes a great sauce for pasta.

Feta

Feta has some serious back story. Food historians think it was made more than 2,000 years ago and was enjoyed by Alexander the Great. It was also mentioned in Homer's epic tale *The Odyssey*.

The crumbly cheese remains the pride and joy of Greece today, eaten for breakfast, lunch and dinner, so it was no surprise the country fought hard for it to be enshrined in the EU's protected food scheme. This was achieved in 2002 when feta was awarded Protected Designation of Origin (PDO) status, meaning that it can only be made in Greece with sheep's milk, plus up to 30 per cent goats' milk.

Made by brining curd for at least two months, feta comes in different styles. One hundred per cent sheep's milk cheeses are richer and sweeter, while those with added goats' milk tend to be whiter and more piquant. Much of the supermarket stuff is brined in metal tanks for the minimum amount of time and has a simple, salty flavour. But feta cheeses that are aged in traditional beechwood barrels for six months to a year are much more interesting, developing fruity and barnyardy flavours, plus a more compact texture. They are lovely with a drizzle of honey and a few thyme or mint leaves.

Plenty of cheeses are similar to feta but can't be labelled as such because of the PDO. Graceburn, made from raw cows' milk by Blackwoods in Kent, is one to look out for. It's marinated in rapeseed (canola) oil, infused with herbs and black pepper and is great whipped or added to salads, if you can resist eating it straight from the jar.

Five cheese macaroni

Serves 6

FOR THE BECHAMEL SAUCE

850ml (1¾ pints) full-fat (whole) milk

120ml (4fl oz) double (heavy) cream (or just add another 120ml/4fl oz of milk)

1 bay leaf

2 garlic cloves, crushed

½ yellow onion, peeled

3 cloves

3 sprigs of thyme

3 sprigs of rosemary

95g (3¼oz) salted butter

75g (2¾oz) plain (all-purpose) flour

120g (4¼oz) Cheddar cheese, grated

120g (4¼oz) Ogleshield cheese, grated (or use raclette)

120g (4¼oz) Lincolnshire Poacher cheese, grated (or use Comté or Gruyère)

2 teaspoons English mustard

pinch of ground nutmeg

salt and pepper

FOR THE HERB CRUMB

50g (1¾oz) salted butter

10g (¼oz) dried rosemary

5g (⅛oz) dried thyme

100g (3½oz) panko breadcrumbs

salt and pepper

FOR THE FIVE CHEESE MACARONI

500g (1lb 2oz) dried macaroni

160g (5¾oz) cooking mozzarella or scamorza cheese, grated

80g (3oz) Old Winchester cheese, grated (or use Parmesan, see note overleaf)

When we opened The Cheese Bar in Camden, I insisted that we use "rotelle" pasta for the macaroni cheese. You know, the wheel-shaped pasta? I thought it was a funny reference to our other business The Cheese Truck.

Turns out, it's quite hard to buy rotelle pasta in the UK, but I wouldn't let it slide. So we imported a pallet of it from Italy, as you do! It lasted about 18 months. Front of house hated me because they had to explain 50 times a day what "rotelle cheese" was. We didn't even sell that much because people were confused by it.

One day, we eventually ran out of it, so our head chef used macaroni on the sly and, guess what? We sold ten times as much because people actually knew exactly what they were ordering! Moral of the story? Keep it simple!

To make the bechamel
- Place the milk, cream, bay leaf, crushed garlic, onion, cloves, thyme and rosemary in a heavy-bottomed saucepan and place over a very low heat and warm for 5–10 minutes. Switch off the heat and allow to infuse for 30–60 minutes. We recommend preparing the rest of the bechamel ingredients, as well as the herb crumb, while this is happening.

- Melt the butter in a large, heavy-bottomed pan over a low heat, then add the flour. Whisk together, ensuring you get into the edges and remove any lumps. Cook out the flour and butter mix over a low-medium heat, whisking constantly, for around 3–5 minutes.

- Remove the solid ingredients from the infused milk liquor with a slotted spoon. Add the milk to the flour and butter mixture over a low-medium heat, continuing to whisk constantly until it has cooked out and is starting to thicken.

- Whisk in the cheeses over the heat until fully incorporated and season with the mustard, nutmeg, salt and pepper, then set aside.

Recipe continues overleaf

To make the herb crumb
- Melt the butter in a saucepan over a low heat, then add the herbs and season. Cook, stirring, for 3–4 minutes to allow the flavours to infuse.

- Take the pan off the heat, add the panko and mix well. Set aside.

To make the five cheese macaroni
- Preheat the oven to 200°C (400°F), Gas Mark 6.

- Bring a saucepan of water to the boil, then add a big pinch of salt and a drizzle of olive oil. Add the macaroni and cook according to the instructions on the packet. You want the pasta to be quite al dente, as it will cook a little further in the oven.

- Drain the macaroni, keeping a little of the cooking water aside. Place the pasta in a large ovenproof dish. Pour over the bechamel, sprinkle over mozzarella and a little of the pasta water to help loosen the sauce, mixing well.

- Spread the breadcrumbs over the top of the pasta and sauce and then top with a very, very generous grating of Old Winchester or Parmesan.

- Bake in the oven for 20 minutes until golden brown and bubbling. Leave to stand for 15 minutes before serving.

Note: Old Winchester is a crystalline, fruity cows' milk cheese from Wiltshire often described as the UK's answer to Parmigiano Reggiano. Parmesan would also work well.

DRINKS PAIRING • DRINKS PAIRING • DRINKS PAIRING • DRINKS PAIRING •

Amontillado sherry

The nutty acidity and higher alcohol content of sherry is more than a match for the mac.

TIME TO GET FUNKY

You can tell a soft washed-rind cheese with your eyes closed. It's the pungent orange rind that gives the game away with powerful aromas ranging from smoked bacon and brown bread to farmyards and sweaty socks. When people talk about smelly cheeses, they are probably talking about washed rinders.

The funky aromas associated with these cheeses come from a special technique used during maturation. As the name suggests, the rind is smeared or "washed" at regular intervals with brine or a mixture of brine and alcohol. By doing this, most yeasts and moulds are killed off, but certain types of bacteria thrive in the salty environment. These bacteria, which are naturally found on human skin (hence the sweaty sock aromas!), proliferate on the rind, making it sticky and smelly with a wonderful colour that can range from peachy to brick red.

It's thought that we have monks to thank for this discovery. In the Middle Ages, monasteries and abbeys across France would make their own cheese and take young cheeses from local farms as part of their taxes. These would be stored in the monasteries' damp, dark cellars – the perfect maturing rooms – where the monks developed techniques such as rind washing.

Some of the most famous cheeses in the world are part of this fragrant family. There are old school classics, such as Stinking Bishop, Epoisses, reblochon and Taleggio, but also a whole new generation, including Rollright, Baronet and Willoughby.

They all have a certain yeasty, savoury character in common, but some are much stronger than others, depending on how much they have been washed and how they have been matured. A ripe Maroilles from northern France is full of fermenting fruit and charcuterie notes, earning it the nickname "old stinker", but Rollright from Gloucestershire is a much gentler proposition with a yeasty and aromatic personality. Plenty of hard cheeses, such as Gruyère and Comté, are also washed in the early days of maturation, before the rind is dried and brushed to give subtle savoury depth to the final cheese.

The bark of a washed-rind cheese is often worse than its bite. A ripe Epoisses is a beast of a cheese on the nose, but beneath its wrinkly terracotta rind, the paste is buttery and mild. When you take a bite of the rind and the interior at the same time (and you really must eat both) the two parts balance each other out in an incredibly satisfying way. It's a cheese that is deeply savoury and soulful and intense.

The moral of the story? Never judge a cheese by its cover.

Celeriac & potato tartiflette

Serves 2 for a blow-out meal or 4 for a light supper

250g (9oz) celeriac (celery root), peeled and sliced 1cm (½-inch) thick

250g (9oz) potatoes, peeled and sliced 1cm (½-inch) thick

drizzle of olive oil

1 yellow onion, thinly sliced

2 garlic cloves, sliced

80ml (2½fl oz) white wine

1 teaspoon chopped thyme

1 teaspoon chopped rosemary

80ml (2½fl oz) double (heavy) cream

350g (12¼oz) Maida Vale cheese (or similar reblochon-style washed-rind cheese), sliced in half horizontally

salt and pepper

pickles, to garnish (optional)

Lots of people think tartiflette is an ancient cheese dish. But in truth it was invented in the 1980s by reblochon makers to increase sales of their fragrant washed-rind cheese, and quickly became one of the world's favourite cheese dishes. Marketing genius before anyone had heard of social media!

We've omitted the lardons traditionally found in tartiflette and given it a twist by adding some celeriac (celery root), as you do.

We use Maida Vale, a reblochon-style cheese, washed in ale, made by Village Maid Cheese in Berkshire. If you can't find it, then reblochon is the obvious alternative, or feel free to use another soft, mild, washed-rind cheese.

- Preheat the oven to 200°C (400°F), Gas Mark 6.

- Put the sliced celeriac (celery root) and potatoes in a saucepan and cover with salted water. Bring to the boil and simmer for around 8 minutes until slightly al dente, as they'll cook a bit more in the oven. Drain straight away and set aside for later.

- While the potatoes and celeriac are cooking, heat the olive oil in a pan over a low heat. Add the onion and gently fry for 5–7 minutes, until soft and translucent. Add the garlic and cook for another couple of minutes. Add the white wine to the pan and allow to reduce for 2 minutes.

- Remove from the heat and add the thyme, rosemary and cream. Pour into an ovenproof dish and mix in the cooked potatoes and celeriac. Top with the sliced cheese, rind up.

- Bake in the oven for 20–25 minutes until the cheese is melted and bubbling.

- Serve immediately with pickles.

SONG PAIRING · SONG PAIRING · SONG PAIRING · SONG PAIRING ·

Da Funk
DAFT PUNK

It's not a washed-rind cheese without the funk.

Smoked Poacher & haggis Scotch egg

Makes 2

200ml (7fl oz) stout, such as Guinness

150ml (5fl oz) HP Sauce or other brown sauce

120g (4¼oz) Smoked Lincolnshire Poacher cheese, finely grated (or use smoked Cheddar)

3 eggs, 1 beaten

iced water

120g (4¼oz) pork mince (ground pork)

80g (3oz) haggis

pinch of black pepper

plain (all-purpose) flour, for dusting

40g (1½oz) breadcrumbs

vegetable oil, for deep-frying

There are few things in life more satisfying than a proper Scotch egg. We're not talking about those clammy, grey supermarket ones here. We mean a crispy Scotch egg fresh from the fryer with a perfectly runny yolk. Add to that a layer of melted smoked cheese and you reach levels of snack perfection. We use Smoked Lincolnshire Poacher – a traditionally oak-smoked cheese that is a cross between Cheddar and Comté. Any smoked Cheddar will also work. Serve with the stout brown sauce.

- Pour the stout into a pan and bring to a simmer. Reduce until you have about a third left. Once reduced, mix 1 part stout to 2 parts HP Sauce for a stout brown sauce that takes a Scotch egg to new plains.

- While the sauce is reducing, make the Scotch eggs: Line a baking sheet with nonstick baking (parchment) paper. Lay out the finely grated Smoked Poacher on the lined tray and allow to come to room temperature, so that it becomes soft and malleable.

- Bring a large pan of water to a steady boil and add the 2 eggs in their shells. Cook for 6 minutes.

- Drain and put the eggs straight into the iced water. When cool, peel the eggs and set aside.

- In a bowl, mix together the pork mince (ground pork), haggis and black pepper. Split the mixture into 2 x 100g (3½oz) patties.

- Lay another sheet of baking parchment on top of the Poacher and flatten the cheese into a sheet with a rolling pin. Then cut 2 small circular patties of the cheese, around 11.5cm (4¼ inches) in diameter.

- The trick to assembling the Scotch egg is to lay out a sheet of cling film (plastic wrap) around 20cm (8-inches) long. Dust it with a layer of flour and place one of the meat patties on top.

Recipe continues overleaf

- Using your hand, flatten it until you get a 12cm (4½-inch) round meat patty. Add to this a layer of cheese, ensuring you get a consistent 3mm (⅛-inch) layer all the way across, leave a 5mm (¼-inch) gap around the edge of the sausage meat and then place one egg in the middle of the cheese.

- Collect up the corners of the cling film and bring together, gently squeezing to completely cover the egg in the sausage meat mix. Ensure all the egg is covered.

- Repeat for the other patty and egg, then chill both in the refrigerator for 1 hour.

- Remove the eggs from the refrigerator and remove the cling film. Dip the balls into the beaten egg and then into the breadcrumbs, ensuring an even coating. Repeat this process until they are fully covered.

- Half-fill a large heavy-bottomed pan with vegetable oil and place over a medium heat until it reaches 180°C (350°F) on a sugar (candy) thermometer. If you don't have a thermometer, test the oil with a cube of bread. It should brown in 30-40 seconds when the oil is at the right temperature. Deep-fry your Scotch eggs for 6 minutes each until they are golden brown.

- Carefully remove from the pan and allow to drain on kitchen paper (paper towels). Serve warm with the brown stout sauce.

Stout

A rich, dark stout meets the haggis and smoked cheese head on.

Baked Tunworth

Serves 2

1 Tunworth, in its box (or use another soft cheese)

2 short sprigs of rosemary

honey

splash of white wine

plenty of fresh sourdough, for dipping

The famous French chef Raymond Blanc once declared Tunworth to be "the Best Camembert in the world". Not bad for a cheese from Hampshire!

Made by Stacey Hedges and Charlotte Spruce near Basingstoke, it's similar to Camembert but is creamier because it's made with whole cows' milk (the traditional French fromage is made with partly skimmed milk). This richness and the fact it comes in a wooden box make Tunworth a particularly good baking cheese, but you could use other mould-ripened soft cheeses for this recipe and mix up the accompaniments (see box).

- Preheat the oven to 200°C (400°F), Gas Mark 6.

- Remove all the labels from the Tunworth box and any plastic wrapping from the cheese. Place the cheese back in the box without the lid on.

- Cut a small cross on the top of the cheese and push in 2 short sprigs of rosemary. Drizzle the cheese with honey and a splash of white wine.

- Place the Tunworth in a small skillet or baking tray. Bake in the oven for 12–15 minutes until the cheese is wobbly and molten in the centre.

- Serve immediately with the sourdough for dipping!

Other baked cheese ideas

Brie-style cheeses like Baron Bigod or Brie de Meaux with Mushroom duxelles (see page 169).

Washed-rind cheeses like Rollright or reblochon with Bacon jam (see page 169).

Soft blue cheeses like Cote Hill Blue or Cambozola with figs and walnuts.

Goats' cheese with Chilli jam (see page 164).

Ricotta with Sun-dried tomato & basil pesto (see page 168).

IN BLOOM

Mouldy food doesn't usually take pride of place on the dinner table. But cheese is a glorious exception. The secret lives of moulds and yeasts play an important role in many cheeses, but none more so than famous softies, such as Camembert, Brie and goats' cheeses.

Whenever you see a flat, bloomy white coat on a soft cheese, you are looking at a living, breathing colony of moulds called *Penicillium camemberti*. If it's an ivory, wrinkly rind, it's probably a delicious yeast called *Geotrichum candidum*. Quite often, the two work together in unison.

That might all sound slightly unsettling, but don't worry. These are perfectly safe and edible types of fungi, and they have been used in cheese for centuries. Added to the milk or sometimes sprayed onto the rinds of cheeses, these delicious moulds and yeasts help transform chalky young cheeses into glorious bundles of silky goo.

The science of how they do this is complicated, but essentially the rind breaks down the cheese underneath, making it softer and runnier and creating complex flavours. In other words, these cheeses ripen from the outside in. White mould-ripened cheeses, such as Brie and Camembert, will ripen all the way to the centre and often have amazing earthy, wild mushroom and cabbage notes. Soft yeast-ripened cheeses, such as wrinkly goat's logs, might not ripen all the way through, but they will usually have a soft layer just beneath the rind (known as the breakdown/creamline), which have similar earthy notes, but also fruity, spicy and grassy aromas, depending on the cheese.

Supermarkets find these cheeses tricky. Without specialist counters and mongers to keep an eye on them, cheeses that become runny make a mess on the shelf. So big dairies have come up with a cunning solution: a Brie that never fully ripens. Known as "stabilized Bries", they are made to be soft and springy without ever getting properly oozy. They're a pale shadow of traditionally made cheeses.

The two questions that everybody asks about these types of cheeses are, "When are they ripe?" and, "Do I eat the rind?"

The answer to the first is a matter of taste. Most people like their Bries gooey all the way to the middle. If the rind has coppery flecks and the interior is bulging like cold quivering custard then you're on the right track. But a minority quite like a thin line of chalk in the heart of the cheese to contrast with the ooze.

If the interior is mainly chalk and the rind is snowy white, it's probably under ripe. At the other end of the scale, if the centre of your cheese has turned to soup, the rind is brown and cracked and it has that sharp chemical smell of ammonia, then it's probably past its best.

When it comes to whether or not to eat the rind, the advice couldn't be simpler. Yes. Always. The rind is an integral part of the cheese and has a lot of flavour. You're missing out on half the experience if you don't eat the mould.

Three cheese & vegetable pasty

Makes 6-8

* You will need a 16-18cm (6-7-inch) plate to cut your pastry around

FOR THE FILLING

125g (4½oz) celeriac (celery root), cut into 2cm (¾-inch) pieces

175g (6oz) butternut squash, cut into 2cm (¾-inch) pieces

125g (4½oz) parsnip, cut into 2cm (¾-inch) pieces

4 teaspoons vegetable oil

160g (5¾oz) red onions, cut into 2cm (¾-inch) pieces

175g (6oz) leek, cut into 2cm (¾-inch) pieces

2 garlic cloves, finely chopped

6 sprigs of thyme

100ml (3½fl oz) water

30g (1 oz) mint, sliced into thin strips

100g (3½oz) harissa

120g (4¼oz) halloumi cheese, cut into 2cm (¾-inch) pieces (see page 134 for more on halloumi)

100g (3½oz) mozzarella cheese, grated

150g (5½oz) Spenwood cheese (or another hard sheep's milk cheese, such as Manchego), grated

salt and pepper

FOR THE PASTIES

flour, for dusting

1kg (2lb 4oz) shortcrust pastry (pie dough)

1 egg or milk, to glaze

House tomato ketchup (see page 45), to serve

Prior to devoting my life to cheese I used to sell pies and pasties at music festivals for a guy called James Stephenson. Without James, I doubt The Cheese Truck would have ever got started. So, I owe James a massive thank you!

Anyway, when we opened the Barge, I said to our head chef that nothing felt more British than a pasty. She took on the challenge of creating a cheese-filled pasty and came up with something special.

Make these pasties in advance, then keep them in the refrigerator until you're ready to wow your friends. Give them a glaze and get them in the oven. Hey presto: heavyweight snacks.

To make the filling

• Preheat the oven to 180°C (350°F), Gas Mark 4 and line a baking tray with nonstick baking (parchment) paper.

• Place the celeriac (celery root), butternut squash and parsnip on the lined baking tray, drizzle with oil and season. Roast for 10–15 minutes. You want them a little hard as they will cook further in the pasty. Set aside to cool.

• Meanwhile, heat a little oil in a medium pan over low heat and cook the onions, leek, garlic and thyme for 8-10 minutes until soft. Set aside to cool.

• In a large bowl, mix the cooked vegetables and remaining ingredients together to make the filling and season to taste.

Recipe continues overleaf

To make the pasties

- Roll out the pastry (pie dough) on a lightly floured surface to around ½cm (¼-inch) thick. Using a plate as a template, cut out 6 x 16-18cm (6-7-inch) discs of pastry.

- Place one sixth of your filling into the centre of each disc. Lightly brush the edge of the pastry with water. Bring the pastry together so the half circles line up, and firmly squeeze the edges together.

- Crimp along the edges of the pasty: starting at one end, push down on the edge of the pastry with your finger and fold over the next bit of pastry along the edge. Hold this bit down with your finger and repeat for the whole length. When you get to the end, you can fold the edge underneath the pasty. Repeat for the remaining pasties.

- When you're ready to bake your pasties, preheat the oven to 210°C (410°F), Gas Mark 7 and line a tray with nonstick baking (parchment) paper.

- Whisk the egg in a small bowl. Or just use milk. Place your pasties on the lined baking tray and, with a pastry brush, glaze the top of the pasties with the egg or milk wash.

- Bake in the oven for 20-25 minutes until the pastry is golden brown and the filling is piping hot.

- Enjoy with a dollop of House tomato ketchup.

Jersey curd tart

Serves 10

* You will need a 23cm (9-inch) fluted tart tin (loose bottomed) and baking beans (pie weights)

FOR THE BOOZY CURRANTS

150g (5½oz) caster (superfine) sugar

150ml (5fl oz) water

1 Earl Grey tea bag

zest of 1 lemon

200g (7oz) currants

30ml (1fl oz) cider brandy or Calvados

FOR THE TART CASE (SHELL)

flour for dusting

250g (9oz) shortcrust pastry block (pie dough)

FOR THE FILLING

750g (1lb 10oz) Jersey curd cheese

160g (5¾oz) icing (confectioners') sugar

3 large (US extra-large) egg yolks

3 large (US extra-large) eggs

60ml (4 tablespoons) cider brandy or Calvados

Yorkshire curd tart is steeped in British dairy history. It was traditionally made by Yorkshire cheesemakers at the end of the day as a way to use up any leftover curds.

The modern version of the recipe requires curd cheese, which is a little like cream cheese, but with a lower fat content and a lactic tang. It's not the easiest ingredient to get hold of, but not impossible. We buy Jersey curd cheese from The Old Cheese Room in Wiltshire, which you can purchase online.

There's also a Polish cheese, called Twaróg, which isn't made with Jersey milk, but is a good alternative and quite widely available in supermarkets. You can also make your own. There are online recipes for curd cheese, which are simple to make. They involve curdling whole milk with lemon juice and draining the whey in a cheesecloth.

To make the boozy currants
• Combine the sugar, water, tea bag and half the lemon zest in a small saucepan and boil over a medium heat until the sugar dissolves, about 3-4 minutes.

• Remove from the heat and add the currants, the other half of the lemon zest and the cider brandy. Stir well. Allow to steep overnight in the refrigerator. These will keep in an airtight container in the refrigerator for 1 week. Remove the currants from the marinade before serving.

To make the tart case (shell)
• Preheat the oven to 180°C (350°F), Gas Mark 4.

• Roll out the pastry on a floured work surface so that there is a sufficient overhang for when you line the tin. Lay the pastry into the tin and make sure you press it into the grooves on the side.

• Prick the bottom of the pastry with a fork, then line with nonstick baking (parchment) paper and baking beans (pie weights).

• Bake in the oven for 20 minutes, then remove the baking beans and cook for another 15 minutes until golden.

• Remove from the oven, and trim the edges of the pastry with a knife so the sides are level with the tray.

Recipe continues overleaf

To make the filling
· Turn the oven down to 160°C (325°F), Gas Mark 3.

· Put the curd cheese and icing (confectioners') sugar in a blender and blend until smooth, or put them in a bowl and beat with a whisk.

· Add the egg yolks, whole eggs and cider brandy to the curd mixture and blend or beat again until smooth.

· Place the baked tart case on a sturdy oven tray, pour in the Jersey curd mixture and bake for 25–30 minutes; the tart should have a slight wobble when cooked.

· Remove from the oven, place on a cooling rack, and leave to completely cool before serving with the boozy currants scattered on the top.

· Your tart will keep for 3 days in the refrigerator.

Alex's ricotta & lemon baked cheesecake

Serves 10

* You will need a 23cm (9-inch) round springform tin

FOR THE BASE

250g (9oz) digestive biscuits (graham crackers)

90g (3¼oz) butter, melted

FOR THE FILLING

500g (1lb 2oz) cream cheese

900g (2lb) ricotta cheese

250g (9oz) caster (superfine) sugar

zest of 2 lemons

pinch of salt

1 teaspoon vanilla bean paste

1 tablespoon cornflour (cornstarch)

3 eggs

Who's Alex? Well, Alex Lambert was our very first employee at The Cheese Truck and put his stamp on the business in the early years. He was there the day we sold our first sandwich, the day we bought our first truckle of Cheddar, and the day we wrote off our first truck on the way back from Glastonbury – but that's another story!

Alex is an artisan baker by trade and this is his take on a classic. We're not reinventing the wheel, but if you secure yourself exceptional ingredients and cook this with care, then you'll have an outstanding cheesecake on your hands.

Top tip: Serve with a dollop of Poached cherries in sherry (see page 165) or Honey lemon curd (see page 172).

To make the base
- Line the base and sides of a 23cm (9-inch) round springform tin with nonstick baking (parchment) paper. The easiest way to do this is by rubbing butter around the sides to help the paper stick.

- Pulse the biscuits (crackers) in a blender or food processor until evenly broken up but not a fine powder. Mix with the butter.

- Press this mixture into the base of the lined tin until it is evenly covered. Refrigerate the base for at least 2 hours.

To make the filling
- Preheat the oven to 180°C (350°F), Gas Mark 4.

- Excluding the eggs, add all the ingredients for the filling to a blender or food processor and blitz together until smooth.

- Still in the blender, beat the eggs in one at a time.

- Take the base out of the refrigerator and pour in the filling.

- Bake for 40–45 minutes until the edges are set and slightly brown and the middle is still slightly wobbly. Don't be over cautious and bake it for longer, it will set as it cools.

- Allow to cool in the tin and then chill overnight.

- Once chilled, remove the outer ring and serve.

AND THE WINNER IS...

It's a scene to thrill the senses. A room the size of an aeroplane hangar filled with more than 4,000 cheeses from all corners of the planet.

Stretching into the distance is every shape, size and colour of cheese imaginable (and some that are not). Shiny drums of Grana Padano the size of car wheels and craggy towers of blue cheese mingle with dainty buttons of goats' cheese and gooey discs of Brie. There are holey Emmenthal cheeses, bouncy balls of buffalo mozzarella and plastic-wrapped blocks of Cheddar, plus all manner of cheeses dusted with ash or paprika and coated in leaves or flower petals.

Framing this kaleidoscope of cheeses is a beguiling aroma, which floats in the air like a particularly pungent perfume. Earthy, savoury and undeniably cheesy, it grabs you by the nose and draws you in to the field of cheese.

This is what greets judges at the World Cheese Awards, an eagerly anticipated annual event that involves cheeses from more than 40 countries being ogled, prodded, sniffed and chewed by some of the most knowledgeable cheese experts on the planet.

More than 250 judges, from cheesemakers and mongers to chefs and food writers, congregate in their white coats, cheese irons (cheese triers) and knives at the ready, to blind judge thousands of cheeses in a single day. The award ceremony moves from country to country. Italy, Spain, Norway and Wales have all hosted in the past, but the aim is always the same: to narrow down the field to find one single winner. In other words, the best cheese in the world (for that year at least).

Set up in 1988 by the UK-based Guild of Fine Food, the event is one of many cheese competitions that take place all over the world. There's the Global Cheese Awards in Frome, Somerset, and the World Championship Cheese Awards in Wisconsin, plus a myriad of national contests, but it's the World Cheese Awards that is seen by many as the most prestigious.

Recent winners of the Supreme Champion title have included a Norwegian Gouda called Fanaost, made on a farm with just 12 cows, and a square Spanish goats' cheese with a line of ash through the middle called Olavidia. Rogue River Blue, a blue cheese from Oregon, wrapped in vine leaves, caused controversy when it won in 2019. That's because the awards were held in Italy that year and the cheese pipped a Parmigiano Reggiano to the title by just one vote. Newspaper headlines across Italy expressed outrage the next day, not just because an Italian cheese had lost, but because it had been beaten by a cheese made in America – a country associated, in the minds of reporters, with orange burger slices rather than award-winning artisan cheese.

Judge and jury

Cheese judging is a serious business that requires all the senses. Judges work in teams and typically have three hours to blind judge around 40 cheeses, so speed is of the essence, but not at the expense of giving each cheese proper attention. A visual inspection to check for faults, such as cracks and slimy rinds, is backed up by much poking and squeezing to check the texture.

Then it's all about the aroma and the flavour, with balance, nuance, complexity and length all key considerations. Only the best are given an award – bronze, silver, gold or the much coveted Super Gold. The best cheeses are put forward

to other judging rounds and are narrowed down to a final 16, which are judged again in front of a live audience with the "super jury" revealing their scores in a game-show-style judging spectacle, until an overall winner is found.

It's not just cheeses that win awards. There are several contests to put cheesemongering skills to the test, from cutting and wrapping to cheese knowledge and customer service. At the Concours National des Fromagers in France, contestants are put through their paces in a series of challenges in front of a live audience. These include creating elaborate cheeseboards that resemble works of art. It's a highly pressurized business that gives cheesemongers the chance to make their name in the industry.

Raw milk rockstars

Cheesemongers are also lauded in the US in the Cheesemonger Invitational (CMI), which is an altogether more raucous affair. Taking place in San Francisco and New York, the biannual contest is a wild and rowdy cheese party. Or as the CMI puts it: "This is a have-to-be-there, FOMO-inducing, adrenaline-pumping cheesesplosion."

Entrants attend two days of educational cheese workshops, before the competition starts with 10 different rounds designed to test their prowess, before the field is narrowed down for the final. This is attended by hundreds of baying cheese fans, wearing T-shirts with slogans such as "raw milk rockstar" and "last night a cheesemonger saved my life". Organizer Adam Moskowitz, a former rapper and DJ turned cheese distributor, MCs the event as his alter ego Mister Moo, complete with cow onesie and gold cow bell. Blind tastings, speed wrapping and left-field drinks pairings are all part of the show with the winner pocketing a $1,000 cheque while hoisting a giant trophy topped with a golden cow.

Never mind celebrity chefs. Cheesemongers are the new rock stars.

GR

ATE

Truffled mushroom eggs

Serves 2

oil, for frying

200g (7oz) mushroom, sliced
(try to get a mix of what's in
season, see introduction)

2 teaspoons confit garlic butter
(see the aligot recipe on page 87)

50ml (2fl oz) double (heavy)
cream

drizzle of truffle oil

juice of ½ lemon

2 eggs

2 thick-cut bread slices, toasted

90g (3¼oz) Spenwood cheese
(or other hard sheep's milk
cheese)

salt and pepper

1 teaspoon chopped parsley,
to garnish

The perfect breakfast in bed, if you're out to impress! Fried eggs
and mushrooms on toast are given a sexy twist with a splash of truffle
oil and a generous grating of cheese.

My favourite mushrooms are Scottish chanterelles, but then I'm a bit
fancy like that. Try to find a mix of mushrooms – wild, button (white),
field and chestnut (cremini) – to add different flavours and textures.

And when it comes to the cheese, we love Spenwood, a hard sheep's
milk cheese from Berkshire. But you could use similar cheeses,
such as Berkswell, Manchego, pecorino or Ossau Iraty.

Whatever you decide, don't skimp and make sure you do both layers
of grated cheese as it really makes the difference.

- In a pan over a high heat, add a drizzle of oil and cook the mushrooms
  for 5 minutes until softened and taking on some colour. When the
  mushrooms are nearly cooked, add the garlic butter and cream to
  the pan and season with salt and pepper. Add a small drizzle of truffle
  oil and the lemon juice, and cook for 1 minute more until the cream
  is bubbling.

- In a second pan, add a drizzle of oil and fry the eggs over medium
  heat for 4 minutes.

- Place the toasted bread on a serving plate and, with a fine grater,
  coat the slice with a thin layer of Spenwood. Top this with the cooked
  mushrooms and then the egg.

- Grate over another thin layer of Spenwood and garnish with
  the parsley.

SONG PAIRING • SONG PAIRING • SONG PAIRING • SONG PAIRING •

Sunday Mornin'
MARGO GURYAN

Breakfast in bed with
a cult pop classic!

Saganaki with honey, lemon & oregano

Serves 2

drizzle of olive oil

2 x 120g (4¼oz) slabs of halloumi cheese

60g (2¼oz) honey

1 lemon, halved

handful of fresh oregano leaves

Saganaki is a Greek dish named after the small cast iron skillet it's served in. It's traditionally made with Kefalograviera, a hard sheep's milk cheese, but there are also versions made with halloumi. In the US, it is sometimes flambéed and is known as "flaming saganaki" because for some reason a restaurant in Chicago thought it needed setting on fire tableside.

With a simple dish you need exceptional ingredients because there is nowhere to hide. So don't skimp on the halloumi. Look for 100 per cent sheep's milk, which is creamier than mixed milk versions.

It's best to serve this sizzling hot in a small cast iron skillet. Otherwise, cook the cheese in a frying pan and get it on plates in front of your hungry guests ASAP.

- Heat the olive oil in 2 small cast iron skillets or a pan over a medium heat until hot but not smoking. Add the halloumi slabs and cook for about 4 minutes until they are golden and crispy on the bottom. Flip the halloumi and repeat on the other side.

- Drizzle the halloumi with honey, squeeze over the lemon juice to taste and scatter over the oregano.

- Serve sizzling hot in the cast iron skillet or pan and enjoy.

Halloumi

A summer barbecue in Britain isn't complete without a hunk of halloumi gently browning on the grill. But this wasn't always the case.

In the early 2000s, halloumi was a niche speciality that was largely unknown among the wider public. The story of how Cyprus' most popular cheese went from cult status to British national treasure is complicated, but interest in Mediterranean food driven by celebrity chefs and people looking to cut down on meat were all part of the plot.

The cheese is protected by EU law and UK trademarks, which means it can be made only in Cyprus and with at least 51 per cent sheep's milk (or a mixture of sheep and goats' milk). Cows' milk can make up the rest, but can never be the main ingredient. The fact that halloumi is so heavily protected has inspired cheesemakers outside Cyprus to come up with ingenious names for similar products, from "squeaky cheese" to Hello Ewe.

Halloumi is made by cooking the curd in whey and salting the cheese either by hand or in brine. It's also often sprinkled with mint. The result is a rubbery texture that does not melt. Instead, it softens and caramelizes when cooked, making it perfect for grilling and frying. The best halloumi is made with 100 per cent sheep's milk – it has a marshmallow texture, plus lots of salty sweetness.

And if you've ever wondered why halloumi squeaks when you eat it, then we have the answer. The cheese is made up of compact proteins, which rub against your teeth when you chew. Now you know!

English Pecorino squash spätzle

Serves 2 generously

FOR THE SQUASH PURÉE

½ small butternut squash
(at least 400g/14oz), skin on

salt

FOR THE SPÄTZLE

85g (3oz) squash purée
(see above)

2 medium (US large) eggs

5g (⅛oz) table salt

110g (3¾oz) plain (all-purpose)
flour

vegetable oil, for coating

TO ASSEMBLE

10g (¼oz) pumpkin seeds

10g (¼oz) pine nuts

60g (2¼oz) confit garlic butter
(see page 87)

5 sage leaves

150g (5½oz) squash purée (see
above)

100g (3½oz) English Pecorino
(or another hard sheep's milk
cheese, see note overleaf)

We opened The Cheese Barge, our 96-foot floating restaurant at Paddington Basin in London, just as lockdown rules relaxed in May 2021. I found myself working there as the general manager for the first 3 months, and this dish was my go-to-dinner EVERY DAY.

Spätzle is a German version of pasta made with a simple egg dough, which has the texture of dumplings when cooked. It's simple to make and cooks in 2 minutes. Perfect for a mid-week dinner.

The key is the consistency of the dough. You want it to be a thick batter but thin enough to pass through a colander with a little push from the spatula. You're looking to make small irregular squiggles!

To prepare the squash purée
- Preheat the oven to 200°C (400°F), Gas Mark 6.

- Remove the seeds from the squash. Season with salt and place in a deep oven tray with a couple of centimetres (about an inch) of water.

- Wrap the tray in nonstick baking (parchment) paper and aluminium foil and bake for about 30–45 minutes, or until soft.

- Remove from the oven and leave to cool. Scrape out the flesh from the skin and mash until smooth (or purée in a blender or food processor).

- You'll need 235g (8¼oz) of purée for the dish – keep the rest in an airtight container for up to 3 days in the refrigerator, or 2 months in the freezer.

To make the spätzle
- Fill a medium pan with salted water and bring to the boil.

- Place 85g (3oz) of the squash purée, the eggs and the salt in a bowl and mix. Save the rest of the purée for later.

- Mix in the flour and vigorously whisk until you have a thick, smooth batter with bubbles on the surface. Use the batter immediately.

- Prepare a bowl of cold water for chilling the spätzle.

- Place a colander over the hot salted water and, working in batches, place some batter into the centre. Slowly move it back and forth with a spatula, so it has time to drop through the holes into the water.

Recipe continues overleaf

- Boil the spätzle for 2 minutes and, when they rise to the top of the water, transfer to the cold water.

- Once you have finished, drain the spätzle and coat in oil so they don't stick together. Set aside.

To bring it all together!
- Preheat the oven 170°C (340°F), Gas Mark 3½.

- Place the pumpkin seeds and pine nuts on a baking tray. Roast until aromatic and golden, about 6-7 minutes. Keep to one side for later.

- Place the confit garlic butter and sage leaves in a frying pan over a low heat until melted.

- Add the spätzle and fry in the butter for a couple of minutes, until they're glossy and warmed through. Add the pumpkin seeds and pine nuts for an additional minute.

- Time to plate up! Dig out 150g (5¼oz) of the squash purée from earlier and spread this in the bottom of a serving dish.

- Transfer the spätzle, pumpkin seeds and pine nuts to the dish, on top of the squash purée.

- Finish by grating a generous helping of English Pecorino over the top, and serve.

Note: English Pecorino is made by White Lake in Somerset. Italian Pecorino Sardo, or other hard sheep's milk cheese, would also work.

DRINKS PAIRING · DRINKS PAIRING · DRINKS PAIRING · DRINKS PAIRING

Spätburgunder

The German name for Pinot Noir. Silky, earthy and with zippy acidity.

Jerusalem artichokes & Cashel Blue cream

Serves 4 as a side dish

FOR THE CASHEL BLUE CREAM

60g (2¼oz) Cashel Blue cheese (or another soft, mild blue cheese)

100g (3½oz) cream cheese

1–2 tablespoons full-fat (whole) milk

FOR THE ARTICHOKES

500g (1lb 2oz) Jerusalem artichokes, scrubbed but not peeled

olive oil, for drizzling

FOR THE HAZELNUT BUTTER

50g (1¾oz) butter

20g (¾oz) hazelnuts, crushed

Confession number 243 of this book: I'd never tried Jerusalem artichokes before Reagan Ellenbroek, our first Head Chef at The Cheese Barge, added them to the menu. I can't get enough of them now. Sweet and nutty when roasted, the knobbly little vegetables are the perfect foil for the creamy, salty tang of Ireland's Cashel Blue cheese. Hazelnut butter takes everything to another level.

To make the Cashel Blue cream

• Break up the Cashel Blue and add it to a blender or food processor with the cream cheese and 1 tablespoon of the milk. Blitz until it makes a smooth silky sauce with the consistency of double (heavy) cream.

• If you need to add more milk, then do it gradually.

To cook the artichokes

• Preheat the oven to 180°C (350°F), Gas Mark 4.

• Place the artichokes on a baking tray and drizzle with oil, giving the tray a shake so that they're evenly coated.

• Roast in the oven for 45–55 minutes until golden and tender.

To make the hazelnut butter

• While the artichokes are cooking, gently heat the butter in a pan over low heat. Add the hazelnuts and allow the butter to warm through, then remove from the heat.

To serve

• Put the artichokes on a plate and drizzle with the hazelnut butter.

• Finally, add a good dollop of the Cashel Blue cream.

Burrata with sage & hazelnut pesto

Serves 1 or 2, depending on how much you love burrata...

FOR THE SAGE AND HAZELNUT PESTO (MAKES 150G/5½OZ)

40g (1½oz) hazelnuts

25g (1oz) fresh sage

50g (1¾oz) Berkswell cheese, grated (or another hard sheep's milk cheese, such as pecorino)

150ml (5fl oz) olive oil, or more to taste

25g (1oz) pumpkin seeds

salt and pepper

TO ASSEMBLE

1 x 400g (14oz) burrata cheese, at room temperature

extra virgin olive oil

sea salt flakes

2 sage leaves

Originally from Puglia, burrata is made by forming a pouch of mozzarella, which is filled with cream and ribbons of more mozzarella. When you cut into the supple white cheese, the filling flows in a way that has inspired millions of Instagram posts.

We buy our burrata from the most glamorous woman in British cheese – Simona di Vietri from La Latteria. She makes it with fresh cows' milk every morning in north London and delivers it to our restaurants straight after.

This is important because burrata is at its absolute best when it is freshly made. At a few hours old the cheese is wonderfully perky, and the flavour is bright and milky. How fresh do you feel after a flight across Europe? So how do you think those balls of Italian cheese feel? Our advice: buy local and get it fresh, if you can.

To make the pesto
- Preheat the oven to 200°C (400°F), Gas Mark 6.

- Place the hazelnuts on a baking tray and roast in the oven for around 10 minutes, until golden.

- Meanwhile, add the sage, cheese and olive oil to a blender or food processor, and blend until consistent.

- Add the hazelnuts and pumpkin seeds to the blender and pulse for a short time – you want the nuts nice and chunky.

- Season the pesto to taste and add a little more olive oil if needed, you want the consistency to be thick.

To assemble the dish
- Place your burrata on top of the pesto. You can break it open or leave this for your guests to do at the table.

- Drizzle the olive oil around the plate and the burrata and top with a sprinkle of sea salt and the sage leaves. This is delicious mopped up with bread.

Creamed spinach with red Leicester crisps

Serves 4 as a solid side dish to share

25g (1oz) red Leicester, finely grated – our preferred is Sparkenhoe

375g (13oz) baby spinach

20g (¾oz) salted butter

½ shallot, finely chopped

1 garlic clove, thinly sliced

125ml (4fl oz) double (heavy) cream

pinch of nutmeg

75g (2¾oz) Old Winchester cheese, grated (this can be swapped out for Parmesan)

salt and pepper

Spinach must be the greatest green of all time: tasty, versatile and filled with iron. If it's good enough for Popeye, it's good enough for us, especially when it comes with red Leicester crisps the colour of a sunset.

- Preheat the oven to 200°C (400°F), Gas Mark 6. Line a baking tray with nonstick baking (parchment) paper.

- Start by making your red Leicester crisps. Spoon evenly spaced 1 tablespoon piles of the finely grated cheese onto the lined baking tray. Bake for 6–8 minutes until golden and crisp. Set aside to cool.

- Bring a large pan of salted water to the boil and add the spinach. Cook for 30 seconds before removing and placing in iced water or running under a cold tap to chill.

- Melt the butter in a frying pan over a medium heat, before adding the shallot and garlic. Cook for 5 minutes until they are soft.

- Add the cream and nutmeg. Bring to the boil, then reduce the heat and allow to simmer for 5 minutes before adding the grated Old Winchester.

- While the cream is simmering, squeeze out as much moisture as possible from the spinach, working in small handfuls, and then roughly chop. Add the spinach to the cream mixture and allow to simmer for another 2 minutes.

- Season the creamed spinach with salt and pepper then serve in a large serving bowl with the red Leicester crisps, and enjoy straight away.

Cauliflower fritters with hot sauce

Serves 4 as a starter

1 medium cauliflower, broken into florets

115g (4oz) Cheddar cheese, grated

115g (4oz) Ogleshield cheese, grated (or use raclette)

90g (3¼oz) plain (all-purpose) flour

1 garlic clove, grated or finely chopped

85ml (6 tablespoons) double (heavy) cream

vegetable oil, for frying

salt and pepper

TO SERVE

soured cream

Apple and habanero hot sauce (see page 44)

Cauliflower has had a makeover in recent years, now appearing on menus as everything from cauliflower steaks to cauliflower wings, or how about cauliflower pizza?

But before it got trendy, there was good old cauliflower cheese, which still stands the test of time and was the inspiration for these fritters. Think of them as cauliflower cheese, but easier to share. Serve them with Apple and habanero hot sauce and plenty of soured cream.

To make the fritters
- Bring a large pan of water to the boil. Add the cauliflower florets and blanch for about 8 minutes until tender. Drain and run under cold water to cool them down. Once cold, mash with a potato masher.

- Mix the grated cheeses together in a large bowl. Add the flour, garlic, salt and pepper and mix well. Add the cream and the mashed cauliflower to the bowl and mix well.

- Shape the mixture into small round patty shapes – you want each one to be about 60g (2¼oz).

To cook
- Heat a frying pan over a medium–high heat and add a thin layer of oil to coat the bottom of the pan.

- Working in batches, cook the fritters for 4 minutes on each side until golden brown and crisp, giving them a little push down with the spatula when you flip them. Don't overcrowd the pan.

- Remove and allow to drain on kitchen paper (paper towels).

- Serve with a pot of soured cream and the hot sauce for dipping.

DRINKS PAIRING · DRINKS PAIRING · DRINKS PAIRING · DRINKS PAIRING ·

American IPA

Refreshingly bubbly and fruity, but with a bitter backbone.

LET'S GET READY TO CRUMBLE

There's more to British cheese than Cheddar. The country's other regional cheeses, sometimes known as "territorials", are often overlooked, but ask a monger for their favourite and there's a good chance they will mention Wensleydale, Cheshire, Lancashire, single Gloucester or Caerphilly.

What unites these cheeses is their crumbly texture. Typically aged for just one to four months, they are younger and zestier than Cheddar, with an open, flaky texture. Indeed, this uniquely British style of cheese is often referred to as the "crumblies".

There are plenty of block versions of these cheeses on supermarket shelves, but they are poor imitations of the true cheeses. Made in a very similar way, often in creameries nowhere near the regions the cheeses are named after, they are too young, too sharp and too bitter.

The original cheeses are a different proposition – elegant, mild and milky with spritzy acidity and subtle savoury notes. Thankfully there are a few traditional cheesemakers who continue to represent their regions with pride.

Kirkham's Lancashire is a good example. Made near Goosnargh, the cheese is the only farmhouse, raw milk Lancashire still being made in the world. It's a wonderful cheese that combines curds from two different days, resulting in a fluffy texture and buttery, tangy flavour.

Over the border, the Appleby family make a raw milk, cloth-bound Cheshire, which has a sparkling acidity and mineral character, while there are several old school Wensleydales to look out for, including Yoredale, Stonebeck and Fellstone. A handful of traditional Caerphillies are still standing, including Gorwydd Caerphilly (pictured), which develops a fudgy texture and earthy flavour beneath its velvety grey rind.

Serve it with a piece of dark (semisweet) chocolate and the world is a better place.

Caerphilly, carrot dip & vadouvan leeks

Serves 4

FOR THE BRAISED LEEKS

130g (4½oz) salted butter

2 teaspoons vadouvan spice

200g (7oz) shredded leeks

FOR THE CARROT DIP

1 sweet potato

3 carrots, peeled and roughly chopped

100g (3½oz) red lentils

salt and pepper

TO ASSEMBLE

4 thin sourdough bread slices

olive oil

140g (5oz) Caerphilly cheese (or a tangy territorial cheese, see note)

pinch of garam masala

This dish uses one of my favourite cheeses – Caerphilly. I'm not talking about those bland plastic-wrapped Caerphillies that supermarkets sell. I'm talking about traditional Caerphilly with a velvet grey rind, crumbly centre, and delicious fudgy texture just beneath the rind.

Vadouvan is a French-Indian spice blend. It has all the spices you'd expect from curry powder but also shallot and garlic. You can find it in Waitrose or online, or replace it with a mild curry powder.

To make the braised leeks
- Melt the butter in a pan over a low heat and add the vadouvan spice. Once the butter is fragrant, add the leeks and cook over a low heat to braise for 45 minutes until the butter has lightly browned and the leeks are softly stewed. Allow to cool and put aside for later.

To make the carrot dip
- Preheat the oven to 200°C (400°F), Gas Mark 6.

- Wrap the sweet potato in aluminium foil and bake in the oven for 45–50 minutes until soft. Once cooked, unwrap and peel off the skin.

- Meanwhile, bring a pan of water to the boil. Add the carrots and boil for 10–15 minutes or until soft. Drain and set aside.

- Bring 300ml (10fl oz) water to the boil. Add the lentils and cook as per the instructions on the packet, then drain.

- Put everything in a blender and blend until smooth. Season to taste with salt and pepper.

To assemble the dish
- Preheat the grill (broiler) to high.

- Prepare the crispbreads by drizzling the sourdough slices with olive oil and placing under the hot grill for 2 minutes on each side until golden brown.

- On a serving plate, smear the carrot dip in a consistent layer. Add the braised leeks on top of the carrot. Crumble the Caerphilly over the top of the dish (including the rind) and add a pinch of garam masala scattered over. Serve with the crispbreads.

Note: We use Gorwydd Caerphilly, but Cheshire or Wensleydale would also work.

Goats' cheese panna cotta with rhubarb

Serves 4

* You will need 4 glass jars or ramekins to serve

FOR THE PANNA COTTA

5g (⅛oz) gelatine leaves

65ml (4 tablespoons) double (heavy) cream

250ml (8½fl oz) full-fat (whole) milk

200g (7oz) fresh goats' cheese

45g (1½oz) caster (superfine) sugar

½ teaspoon vanilla extract

ice

FOR THE RHUBARB COMPOTE

200g (7oz) rhubarb, trimmed and cut into 2.5cm (1-inch) pieces

35g (1¼oz) caster (superfine) sugar

4g (⅛oz) honey

2 tablespoons water

zest of ½ orange

Don't fear using goats' cheese in a dessert. It adds body and a sharp tang in a similar way that cream cheese does in a cheesecake.

You want a goats' cheese that doesn't overpower the creaminess of the panna cotta, but still has a noticeable tang. A young goats' cheese, which tastes lemony and mineral-like and hasn't developed any of the goat-like, animal notes of more mature cheeses, is perfect. Good British ones that work well include Sinodun Hill, Rosary or White Lake's firm goats' curd.

To make the panna cotta
- Soak the gelatine leaves in cold water to soften.

- Gently heat all the other ingredients (except the ice) in a pan over medium heat and whisk until completely smooth and steaming. Don't let the mix boil.

- Add in the drained gelatine and whisk until melted and incorporated.

- Transfer the mixture from the pan to a bowl, and place this over the bowl of ice. Continue to whisk until it comes to room temperature.

- Pour equal amounts of the mixture into each glass jar or ramekin and cover.

- Chill in the refrigerator until set (about 2-4 hours).

To make the compote
- Add all the ingredients to a pan over a low heat.

- Cook for 10-20 minutes, stirring regularly, until the rhubarb has softened and the liquid has reduced.

- Allow to cool before putting in the refrigerator.

To serve
- Spoon 1 tablespoon of the compote on top of each panna cotta and keep in the refrigerator until needed.

Note: The leftover rhubarb compote is lovely on cereal, in porridge or used as an accompaniment for oily fish, such as mackerel.

SONG PAIRING · SONG PAIRING · SONG PAIRING · SONG PAIRING ·

Voodoo Ray
A GUY CALLED GERALD

That lemony sharp goats' cheese and tart rhubarb calls for a bit of acid house.

Stilton & caramelized walnut gelato

Makes approx. 10 servings

350ml (12fl oz) full-fat (whole) milk

200ml (7fl oz) double (heavy) cream

pinch of salt

100g (3½oz) Stilton cheese

175g (6½oz) caster (superfine) sugar

5 egg yolks

5 teaspoons water

100g (3½oz) walnuts

tawny port, to serve

This is our riff on affogato, except instead of coffee we heavily encourage you to pour a shot of tawny port over the gelato.

La Gelatiera in London makes this gelato for us, so we asked them to contribute the recipe to the book. We're good at a few things, but we leave making gelato to the pros!

La Gelatiera is a family business, which has shops across London and they're as passionate about gelato as we are about cheese. They hand-make their gelato fresh every day using the best seasonal ingredients and organic dairy produce.

- In a pan over medium heat, heat up the milk and cream with the salt. Once the mixture starts to steam, take it off the heat and crumble in the Stilton, continuously stirring until the cheese is fully melted.

- In a bowl, beat together 150g (5½oz) of the sugar and the egg yolks until they have a pale-light consistency.

- Slowly pour the hot mixture of milk and cream on top of the egg yolks and sugar, whisking vigorously throughout. Once fully incorporated, return the mixture to the pan and put over a low heat. Keep stirring until the mixture is hot and coats the back of a wooden spoon.

- Place the mixture in the refrigerator for 2 hours to bring down the temperature. Once the mixture has cooled, place in an airtight freezerproof container and place in the freezer.

- In the meantime, place the remaining 25g (1oz) sugar and measured water in a pan over a medium heat. Once the sugar starts to brown, add the walnuts and mix well. Keep stirring until the walnuts are nicely coated. Remove from the heat and place on nonstick baking (parchment) paper to cool. Once cooled, roughly chop and set aside.

- After 2 hours, check on the mixture in the freezer; when it starts to thicken, fold in the caramelized walnuts.

- Leave overnight in the freezer to firm up.

- To serve, remove the gelato from the freezer for 5–10 minutes to soften. In a rocks glass or sundae glass, add a scoop of gelato and serve, with a small measure of port to pour over affogato-style!

Roasted plums, ricotta & ginger crumb

Serves 4

FOR THE ROASTED FRUIT

8 ripe plums, halved and stone removed

45g (1½oz) sugar

4 star anise, ground

FOR THE GINGER CRUMBLE

Makes 8 biscuits; you can crumble a couple for this recipe and eat the rest, or store in a airtight container for up to a week

90g (3¼oz) salted butter

75g (2¾oz) light soft brown sugar

115g (4oz) golden syrup

200g (7oz) plain (all-purpose) flour

½ teaspoon ground cinnamon

2½ teaspoons ground ginger

½ teaspoon ground cloves

TO SERVE

320g (11½oz) ricotta cheese

drizzle of honey

This dessert is about as easy as it comes and has endless variations. We've used fresh ricotta (try to find Westcombe Dairy's light and airy Somerset Ricotta) but you could easily use mascarpone, whipped goats' curd, crème fraîche or Greek yogurt.

For the fruit, some of our favourites are pears, peaches, plums, cherries, nectarines and figs. You can play around with the spices; add cinnamon, cloves or even a drizzle of honey and some sweet wine or port before you roast them.

We make a ginger crumb to go on top, but you could add pistachios, walnuts, flaked slivered almonds, granola or even chocolate.

To make the roasted fruit
- Preheat the oven to 200°C (400°F), Gas Mark 6. Line a baking tray with nonstick baking (parchment) paper.

- Toss the plums in the sugar, lay on the lined baking tray and sprinkle over the star anise. Bake for 20–25 minutes, until soft and tender – not mushy and falling apart.

To make the ginger crumble
- Preheat the oven to 140°C (275°F), Gas Mark 1. Line a baking tray with nonstick baking (parchment) paper.

- Heat the butter, sugar and golden syrup in a small pan over a low heat until the butter has melted.

- Place all the dry ingredients in a large bowl. When everything in the pan is melted, pour over the dry ingredients, and mix well.

- Leave the mixture to cool for a bit, then roll into 8 balls, flatten to 1cm (½-inch) thick and place on the lined baking tray. Bake for 40 minutes.

- Remove and allow to cool; the biscuits will firm up as they cool.

- When cool, crumble to biscuits with your hands until your desired texture is achieved.

To serve
- In 4 individual bowls, add 80g (2¾oz) ricotta, then top with a few halves of plum, a sprinkle of the crumb and a drizzle of honey. Dig in!

HOW TO EAT CHEESE

We've all seen wine experts doing their thing. Swirling and sniffing and slurping and spitting. Well, there's a similar process for tasting cheese. Not the swirling (that's hard to do with cheese) and hopefully not the spitting (that would be gross). But there is a step-by-step method to get to know a wedge properly.

You probably don't want to initiate a full professional tasting when you break out the cheeseboard, but it's definitely worth borrowing a few tips from the experts to get maximum pleasure from your fromage.

On your marks

The first thing, and we cannot stress this enough, is to get your cheese to room temperature. It's the single most important thing you can do to fully appreciate the full deliciousness of a cheese.

Cold kills flavour, so inhaling cheese straight from the refrigerator is like going to a gig with ear muffs on. You lose the high notes and harmonies, while even the loudest flavours will be muted. Ideally, take it out an hour before and keep it wrapped until the last minute, so the face doesn't dry out.

If you want to go full cheese geek, then avoid powerful flavours before you taste. That means laying off the double espressos and chewing gum. And don't overdo the perfume. Strong fragrances, scented soaps and handwashes can mess with your sense of smell. Conversely, palate cleansers are helpful – water, apples and crackers are good for rebooting the palate between mouthfuls.

Eyes on the prize

Never judge a cheese by its cover, but you can spot clues by giving it a quick once over.

If the cheese has a rind, it's worth checking that there aren't cracks, bruises or bare patches – signs that it has dried out or been bashed about. The interior of the cheese (known as the "paste") can also tell you a lot. Is it consistent or are there unexpected cracks or holes? If it's a soft, bloomy rinded cheese, is it evenly broken down and gooey? Has it only softened under the rind or all the way to the middle?

Cows' milk cheeses, especially those made in the summer when the cows are at pasture, are often golden in colour thanks to an orange pigment in grass called beta-carotene, which gives their milk a sunset glow. Sheep, goats and buffaloes absorb the pigment, so their milk and cheeses tend to be much whiter in comparison.

Squeeze your cheese

Don't be shy. Texture is important in cheese, so it's perfectly fine to feel your cheese. If the paste has a fluffy or crumbly texture – think soft goats' logs or Wensleydale – that suggests the flavour might be yogurty or citrussy.

Rubbery, more pliable cheeses, such as young Gouda and Edam, are likely to be sweeter and nuttier. If it's dry and crystalline (aged Gouda and Parmigiano), it will likely taste more savoury and intense in flavour. For ripened soft cheeses, such as Camembert and Brie, a thin chalky layer in the middle is okay, but bulging goo is best.

What's your flavour?

Many of the steps outlined opposite are covered by something called the "structured approach to tasting cheese" – a system developed by the cheese education body the Academy of Cheese.

Set up in 2017 by Devon Cheddar maker Mary Quicke, along with other notables of British cheese, such as the Guild of Fine Food and Paxton & Whitfield, the organization teaches qualifications culminating in Master of Cheese – the ultimate ambition for any self-respecting cheese geek.

A colour-coded tasting wheel and a flavour "tree" are important parts of the system, each listing different families of flavours and more detailed words to describe every type of cheese. These range from the obvious – mushroom, cream and nut – to the wild and wacky. Toast, rubber and human are some of the more eye-catching terms, not to mention baby sick, smoked fish, sweat and tears.

The Academy of Cheese is by no means the only organization to have devised flavour wheels. There are several created by universities, while the body that represents Comté cheesemakers in France has a Wheel of Aromas that contains 83 common descriptors for the hard, Alpine cheese. These include horse, cow manure, steamed potato and coffee with milk.

These kinds of flavour charts are really useful when you're trying to find the right vocabulary to describe what's happening in your mouth, nose and brain as you chew.

Recognizing specific flavours is not always easy, so having the written words to hand can help steer you in the right direction.

On the nose

Slice from the centre to the rind so that you have a cross-section of the cheese and can smell and taste every part. The middle of a cheese will taste quite different to just beneath the rind, so no cutting the nose off a wedge.

There's a good chance that the aromas of a cheese will also come through when you taste. So give that piece of cheese a big old sniff.

For mould-ripened, blue and washed-rind cheeses you might get a touch of ammonia. It's a sharp, chemical smell that can be reminiscent of cleaning products or stale urine. Either way, a delicate waft of ammonia is no bad thing – it suggests the cheese is ripe. But if your cheese honks like a back-street alley behind a nightclub then it's probably over ripe.

Aromas of plastic and soggy cardboard can also be signs of faults in cheese, but don't be put off by strong smells. Washed-rind cheeses in particular give off a lot of funky fragrances – farmyard, sweaty socks and smoked bacon – but they are often less assertive when you take a bite.

Chew it over

Once you do finally tuck in, then take your time. Chew slowly and breathe so the flavours come through and develop on your palate. And try different parts of the cheese. There are different flavours and textures near the rind compared to the heart of the cheese. The important thing is to take your time. Some cheeses might give you a big hit of flavour up front, but others reveal themselves in stages over a longer period.

Picking individual flavours is not always easy. A flavour wheel is a really useful tool. A good tip is to begin with the five basic tastes – sweet, salty, acidic, bitter and savoury. Then use them as diving boards to more complex individual flavours.

So if a cheese is savoury, it might lead you to pick a roast beef or bacon fat note. If there's a touch of dairy sweetness, it might be caramel or butterscotch. And once you start picking up acidity in a cheese, that might lead you to think of lemons or yogurt.

The more you taste, the better you become at translating flavours into words.

Do I eat the rind?

The short answer is "yes". Rinds are part of the cheese and are not going to do you any harm. They often hold a lot of flavour, so give them a go and make up your own mind.

It's definitely a good idea to eat the rinds of bloomy and wrinkly rinded cheeses, such as Brie or goats' cheese logs, and the peachy, pungent skin on a washed-rind cheese. They are packed with flavour. The same goes for the natural rinds on young blue cheeses.

For longer aged cheeses with dry, dusty rinds, such as Cheddar and Comté, the choice is up to you. If you don't like the rind, then nibble as close as you can – there are lots of interesting notes just beneath. Similarly, the thick hard exterior of Parmesan is pretty impenetrable, but you can pop it into soups and stews to add an umami hit.

It goes without saying (but we'll say it anyway) that you shouldn't eat the wax, cloth or plastic coating on some cheeses. And best to lay off the leaves and bark that others are wrapped in, although the nettles on the outside of Cornish Yarg are delicious.

WHEN CHEESE GOES BAD

Five common cheese faults:

1. Ammonia

Detecting a hint of ammonia when you smell a soft cheese, such as Brie or Epoisses, is okay, but if you're getting a persistent, strong and sharp hit of stale urine, it's probably over ripe and past its best.

2. Cracks

Cracks in the rind of cheeses, which can also continue into the paste, are a sign the cheese has dried out in the maturing room, cheese counter or refrigerator. If you can, cut the offending sections away and make sure to wrap tightly.

3. Bruises

Cloth-bound Cheddars or Stiltons that are not salted properly or are mishandled develop dark mouldy areas, known as bruises, which don't taste great. Again, just cut away.

4. Bitterness

Under ripe cheeses can be bitter. This might be because the proteins in the cheese haven't broken down properly. Young and overly thick white rinds on soft cheeses can also have the same problem. Leaving them a little longer in the refrigerator may help.

Be careful though. Some Iberian cheeses, such as Torta de Barros and Azeitão, are meant to be bitter. They are made with rennet derived from thistles, which gives a pleasantly acerbic character.

5. Light damage

Does your cheese look washed out and smell of crayons and soggy cardboard? It might be that it's been sitting in direct sunlight or under powerful lights, which leads to something called light oxidation. This results in unpleasant aromas and a bleached appearance. Return to the shop.

CHEESEBOARDS

According to conventional wisdom, the secret to creating a killer cheeseboard is variety. Mix up textures, ages and styles and there will be something for everyone.

It's why so much Brie, Cheddar and Stilton is sold at Christmas. These three cheeses combine a pleasing mix of colours and textures, from white and oozy, through golden and dense to blue and crumbly. If you want to diversify even further, add a goats' or sheep's cheese. And make room for other styles, such as sticky and stinky washed rinds and crystalline Goudas.

These are sensible rules to follow for cheeseboard success, but rules are made to be broken. So there's nothing stopping you from serving a vertical tasting of the same cheese at different ages. Why not try five Cheddars from one farm, from mild to vintage and everything in between?

Or you could go seasonal and have a stunning selection of sheep's and goats' cheeses in the spring, when the milk is at its best. You could even tear up the rule book completely and serve a giant hunk of just one delectable cheese for the whole table to dig into and discuss.

Wedges and wood

Whatever you decide, there are a few other rules worth following. We make this point elsewhere in the book, but it's worth repeating: allow your cheeses to come to room temperature by taking them out of the refrigerator an hour or so before you eat, and they will taste so much better. Another good tip is to buy decent-sized pieces of cheese, so they keep well in the refrigerator and look generous on the table.

In terms of quantities, a decent slice of cheese weighs around 30–35g (1–1¼oz), so for a light, three-cheese cheeseboard, you're looking at about 100g (3½oz) per person. But if the cheese is the main attraction, it's probably best to go for 175g (6oz) per person, or more. Slice the cheeses from the centre to the rind so that everyone has a full cross section of the cheese and an equal amount of rind (see page 192 for more cutting tips).

What you serve your cheeses on comes down to personal taste and aesthetics. Slate, marble, wooden boards or good old plates are just fine. Slates are fun because you can write the name of the cheese on them in chalk, while there are some beautiful boards out there, made from bamboo and olive woods, in various shapes: thick blocks, rounds and planks.

If you do use wooden boards, don't put them in the dishwasher or soak them. They will warp and crack. Wash with warm soapy water and then dry immediately. An occasional rub down with food-grade mineral oil will keep them in tip-top condition.

It's also a good idea to provide a separate knife for each cheese (see pages 190–1 for the different types), so there's no cross contamination. If a knife has just been plunged into a ripe Brie and is then used on a dainty goats' cheese, you'll end with a pretty funky goats' cheese. Similarly, try not to mix up wrappers when you put the cheese back in the refrigerator, to stop moulds and yeasts jumping from one cheese to another.

Beyond crackers and chutney

We don't do edible flowers. The same goes for kiwis and twigs of rosemary. Elaborate grazing platters piled high with fruits and flowers might look pretty on Instagram, but these additions are just a distraction from what's really important: the cheese.

That's not to say you can't be creative when it comes to accompaniments. We love crackers and chutney with cheese, but plenty more can be done with the bits on the side. Lots of foods can be paired with cheese, but the point is whatever you match should lift the experience and take it in exciting new directions.

Picking a flavour in a cheese and complementing it with something similar is a good tactic. The fruity flavour of Gouda with roasted pineapple, for example. Sometimes contrasts work well, like the salty kick of blue cheese with a sweet chocolate brownie. Then there are those curveball matches which we still don't understand. On paper, Turkish delight and goats' cheese should not work, but put them together and they strike up a weird and wonderful combination of floral and herbaceous notes.

Over the coming pages, we've brought together some of our favourite cheeses with accompaniments that have proved hugely popular over the years. There's also advice on which wines and other drinks to serve with cheese.

But they are just suggestions and ideas. There are no rules when it comes to eating cheese. Your way is the best way.

OLD SCHOOL CHEESEBOARD

These British cheeses have stood the test of time for a reason. Cheddar, Wensleydale and Stilton are rooted in the history and geography of the counties where they are made, while Dorstone and Waterloo are veterans of the British cheese renaissance.

1. Dorstone + Chilli jam
This wrinkly, ashed goats' cheese made by Neal's Yard Creamery in Herefordshire has a fluffy texture and bright citrussy flavour. A dash of chilli jam adds fragrant heat and vibrant colour.

2. Montgomery's Cheddar + Grape mustard
The Montgomery family has been making cloth-bound Cheddar for three generations in Somerset. It's a proper Cheddar with a brothy bite, which dovetails with the sweet spice of grape mustard.

3. Cropwell Bishop Stilton + Port-soaked golden raisins
Port and Stilton are natural allies because the powerful fortified wine stands up to the spicy blue. The same is true of port-soaked raisins, which are sweet and plump, and create a pleasing contrast with the salty, savoury cheese from Nottinghamshire.

4. Waterloo + Honeyed garlic
Berkshire-based Village Maid Cheese makes Waterloo with extra creamy Guernsey milk, which gives a richness and golden hue. A drizzle of garlicky honey marries with the buttery sweetness and picks up on earthy notes near the rind.

5. Yoredale + Poached cherries in sherry
There's a lactic tang to this traditional raw milk Wensleydale from the Curlew Dairy in Yorkshire, which combines beautifully with soft, boozy cherries. Think grown-up cherry yogurt.

Chilli jam

Makes approx. 400g (14oz)

500g (1lb 2oz) red (bell) peppers, deseeded and chopped

110g (4oz) fresh red chilli, chopped

4 garlic cloves, chopped

10g (¼oz) fresh root ginger, peeled and chopped

135g (4¾oz) honey

135g (4¾oz) caster (superfine) sugar

100ml (3½fl oz) red wine vinegar

- Place the peppers, chilli, garlic and ginger into a food processor and blend well to a paste.

- Add the paste, along with the honey, sugar and red wine vinegar, to a heavy-bottomed pan and bring to a simmer. Gently simmer until it starts to caramelize, about 30–40 minutes.

- Reduce the heat and gently cook for 20 minutes, until it turns a deep red colour and has a sticky consistency. Transfer to a clean airtight container and allow to cool before sealing. It will keep for 2 weeks in the refrigerator.

Alternative cheese pairings: Brie (France), halloumi (Cyprus), Wensleydale (UK)

Grape mustard

Makes approx. 350g (12oz)

100g (3½oz) brown mustard seeds

60ml (4 tablespoons) red wine vinegar

125g (4½oz) grape molasses

½ teaspoon ground cinnamon

½ teaspoon table salt

¼ teaspoon ground cloves

⅛ teaspoon ground ginger

2 tablespoons red wine

40ml (3 tablespoons) water

- In a pan over a medium heat, lightly toast the mustard seeds until fragrant.

- Mix together the toasted mustard seeds and all the remaining ingredients in an airtight container and leave to stand for 48 hours.

- Divide the mixture in half. Transfer one half to a blender or food processor and blend until smooth. Stir back into the rest of the mixture.

- This will keep in an airtight container in the refrigerator for 2 weeks.

Alternative cheese pairings: bergkäse (Germany), Comté (France), Gouda (Holland)

Port-soaked golden raisins

Makes approx. 300g (10½oz)

125ml (4fl oz) ruby port

½ teaspoon vanilla bean paste

70g (2½oz) icing (confectioners') sugar

1 star anise

2 teaspoons lemon juice

160g (5¾oz) golden raisins

- Put the port, vanilla, icing (confectioners') sugar, star anise and lemon juice into a pan and bring to the boil. Add all the raisins, turn the heat down and simmer for 4 minutes.

- When cooked, allow to cool and then place into an airtight container. Leave to soak in the refrigerator, ideally overnight. These will keep in an airtight container in the refrigerator for 2 weeks.

Alternative cheese pairings: Crozier Blue (Ireland), Lancashire (UK), Vignotte (France)

Honeyed garlic

Makes approx 100g (3½oz)

4 heads of garlic

olive oil

honey

- Preheat the oven to 180°C (350°F), Gas Mark 4.

- First cut off the top off the heads of garlic so the inner cloves are exposed. Drizzle olive oil over the top of the garlic heads and then wrap them together in aluminium foil. Roast in the oven for 45 minutes until soft.

- Allow to cool, then carefully remove the cloves and place in a bowl.

- Use a spoon to mash up the cloves until you have a smooth paste.

- Weigh the paste: you want 30g (1oz) of honey per 50g (1¾oz) of garlic paste. Add the honey to the paste and mix until smooth and consistent.

- This can be kept in the refrigerator for up to 1 week.

Alternative cheese pairings: Camembert de Normandie (France), Harbison (USA), Monte Enebro (Spain)

Poached cherries in sherry

Makes approx. 400g (14oz)

1 teaspoon cornflour (cornstarch)

250g (9oz) fresh pitted cherries

175ml (6fl oz) sweet sherry

50g (1¾oz) icing (confectioners') sugar

juice of 1 lemon

- First step is to dust the cornflour (cornstarch) onto a plate, then roll those little cherries until they are nicely coated all over.

- Add the sherry and icing (confectioners') sugar to a small pan. Bring just to a boil, then simmer until it has reduced by half, about 5–10 minutes.

- Add the cherries, put a lid on the pan, reduce the heat to low and poach for 5–10 minutes until soft.

- Add the lemon juice and you're good to go! These will keep in an airtight container in the refrigerator for up to 1 week.

Alternative cheese pairings: Bonnet (UK), Bonne Bouche (USA), Manchego (Spain)

NEW WAVE CHEESEBOARD

A new generation of producers have taken British cheese in exciting new directions in recent years, abandoning traditional styles and inventing new wave cheeses that defy categorization.

1. Pevensey Blue
+ Chocolate & hazelnut brownie

Stilton and fruit cake are not the only cheese and cake combo in town. A square of bitter-sweet brownie with Pevensey Blue is a very fine thing. The Sussex cheese started life as a homage to Gorgonzola, but has developed into its own cheese that is firmer and more savoury.

2. Rachel + Sundried tomato
& basil pesto

There's an intensity to sundried tomato pesto that demands a cheese with character. Step forward Rachel – a washed-rind, goat Gouda from Somerset that is sweet, nutty and floral with a funky rind.

3. Yarlington + Bacon jam

This pudgy cheese from Gloucestershire is so called because the cheese is rubbed in cider made with Yarlington apples during maturation. This creates farmyardy flavours, as well as fruity, smoky and meaty notes, which are accentuated with a generous helping of bacon jam.

4. Winslade + Mushroom duxelles

This hybrid cheese from Hampshire is partly inspired by French *fromages* Vacherin and Camembert. Encircled by a spruce band, it has a glossy interior full of double (heavy) cream and mushroom notes, which are turbo-boosted by a dollop of mushroom duxelles.

Chocolate & hazelnut brownie

Makes 1 tray of brownies

250g (9oz) salted butter, cubed, plus a little extra for greasing the tray

250g (9oz) dark (semisweet) chocolate

4 eggs

240g (8½oz) caster (superfine) sugar

150g (5½oz) plain (all-purpose) flour

170g (6oz) white chocolate, roughly broken up

60g (2¼oz) hazelnuts, roasted and crushed

• Preheat the oven to 170°C (340°F), Gas Mark 3½ and lightly grease and line a 20 x 20cm baking tray with non-stick baking (parchment) paper.

• Set a heatproof bowl over a pan of hot water, ensuring the bowl does not touch the water. Add the butter and chocolate and melt together.

• In a separate bowl, whisk the eggs and sugar until thick and fluffy.

• Add the chocolate mix to the egg mix and sift in the flour. Fold in the white chocolate and hazelnuts.

• Pour the mixture onto the lined tray and bake in the oven for about 30 minutes, or until a knife poked into the centre comes out clean.

• Allow to cool completely before cutting into small 3cm (1-inch) squares. It will keep for 5 days in an airtight container.

Alternative cheese pairings: Bayley Hazen Blue (USA), Fourme d'Ambert (France), Caerphilly (UK)

Sundried tomato & basil pesto

Makes approx. 400g (14oz)

200g (7oz) sundried tomatoes

½ bunch of basil, leaves picked

40g (1½oz) pine nuts, toasted

40g (1½oz) Berkswell cheese, grated – Parmesan or a hard ewe's milk cheese would also work

90ml (6 tablespoons) oil (use the oil from the sundried tomatoes and/or olive oil)

• Place everything but the oil into a food processor and blend – you want it to be a chunky consistency.

• Add the oil a little at a time, blending between additions, until the correct consistency is achieved; it should be chunky but still smooth. This will keep in the refrigerator for up to a week.

Alternative cheese pairings: feta (Greece), Mozzarella di Bufala Campana (Italy), Ossau-Iraty (France)

Bacon jam

Makes approx. 500g (1lb 2oz)

250g (9oz) bacon mince (ground bacon) or bacon lardons

1 yellow onion, finely diced

200ml (7fl oz) strong coffee

200ml (7fl oz) cider vinegar

150g (5½oz) dark soft brown sugar

50g (1¾oz) black treacle

• In a heavy-bottomed pan over a medium-high heat, fry the bacon for 10-12 minutes until golden. Remove the bacon and set aside.

• Return the pan to a low heat and use the fat left from the bacon to gently sweat the onions until soft and translucent, about 10 minutes. Don't allow them to colour!

• Once the onions are cooked, add the bacon back in along with all the remaining ingredients.

• Bring to a boil and then reduce the heat and allow the mixture to gently simmer, stirring every few minutes, until it has reduced to a jammy consistency, about 25 minutes. Be aware as the jam cools it will become thicker, so don't over reduce.

• Remove from the heat and allow to cool. Store in an airtight container in the refrigerator for up to 2 weeks. It's wonderful on burgers (see page 52), stirred into pasta sauces or just spread on buttered toast.

Alternative cheese pairings: St Cera (UK), Gubbeen (Ireland), Hooligan (USA)

Mushroom duxelles

Makes approx. 400g (14oz)

drizzle of oil

2 shallots, finely chopped

400g (14oz) oyster mushrooms, sliced into strips

55ml (2fl oz) white wine

25ml (5 teaspoons) white wine vinegar

60ml (4 tablespoons) double (heavy) cream

20g (¾oz) salted butter

2-3 sprigs of parsley, finely chopped

¼ bunch of tarragon

salt and pepper

• In a pan, heat the oil over a medium heat and sauté the shallots for 5 minutes until soft.

• Add the mushrooms and cook for 10-15 minutes until soft and all the moisture is gone.

• Add the wine and white wine vinegar and bring to a simmer, then reduce until the liquid has completely evaporated.

• Take off the heat and mix in the cream and butter, then leave to cool.

• Once cool, add the parsley and tarragon, and season with salt and pepper.

• This will keep in an airtight container for 1 week.

Alternative cheese pairings: Chaource (France), Finn (UK), Cooleeney (Ireland)

DAINTY + DELICATE CHEESEBOARD

You don't have to shout to be heard. Some of our favourite cheeses are subtle and mild with complex flavours that require patience. They are particularly good in the spring and summer when warmer temperatures call for lighter, fresher cheeses.

1. Ticklemore + Honey lemon curd

There's nothing quite like Ticklemore. Made in a hexagonal, flying saucer shape, this semi-hard goats' cheese from Devon has a bloomy white coat, flaky texture and zingy, floral flavour. Lemon curd adds to its zesty charms.

2. Beenleigh Blue + Poached pears

Not all blue cheeses blow your socks off. This sweet, minerally sheep's milk blue from Devon is a case in point. Poached pears are perfect for coaxing out its delicate fruity flavour.

3. Gorwydd Caerphilly + Charred leeks

Gorwydd (pronounced "gor-with") Caerphilly from Somerset is three cheeses in one thanks to a lemony and crumbly core, a softer earthy layer close to the surface, and an edible rind that is mushroomy and musty. The sharp bite of charred leeks cuts through all three.

4. Sinodun Hill + Honeycomb

A pyramid-shaped goats' cheese from Oxfordshire, Sinodun Hill has a remarkable whipped-cream texture and mouth-coating creaminess. The sweet crunch of honeycomb is a fabulous contrast.

Honey lemon curd

Makes approx. 400g (14oz)

zest and juice of 4 lemons

200g (7oz) honey

100g (3½oz) unsalted butter

3 eggs and 2 egg yolks, beaten

- Fill a small pan with about 8cm (3 inches) of water, place over a medium heat and bring to a gentle boil.

- Put the zest and juice of the lemons, the honey and the butter into a small metal bowl that is larger than your small pan.

- Place the bowl over the pan of water, ensuring it doesn't touch the water and gently whisk until the butter and honey have melted together.

- Add the eggs to the bowl and continue gently whisking till the mixture has thickened to a custard-like consistency, about 8–10 minutes. Do not stop whisking, otherwise the mixture will scramble.

- Once you have the correct consistency, take off the heat and store in a sterilized jar or airtight container in the refrigerator for up to 2 weeks.

Alternative cheese pairings: Bix (UK), Brillat-Savarin (France), Mt Tam (USA)

Poached pears

Makes 4

650ml (1⅓ pints) water

1 cinnamon stick

3 star anise

2 cloves

zest of 1 lemon

160g (5¾oz) caster (superfine) sugar

4 conference pears, peeled and cut into quarters

- Place the measured water, spices, lemon zest and sugar in a large pan and bring to the boil. When the sugar has dissolved, add the pears, and then simmer for around 45 minutes, until tender but not too soft.

- Leave to cool and store in an airtight container in the refrigerator for up to 2 weeks.

Alternative cheese pairings: Gorgonzola (Italy), Roquefort (France), Parmigiano Reggiano (Italy)

Charred leeks

Makes 1 charred leek

1 leek, sliced into rings

olive oil

sea salt flakes

- We don't use oil for cooking in this recipe, so simply add the leeks to a hot dry pan over a medium–high heat and allow to cook for 10–15 minutes until nicely charred.

- When cooked, take off the heat and add a drizzle of olive oil and a sprinkle of sea salt.

Alternative cheese pairings: Cheshire (UK), Bijou (USA), Sainte-Maure de Touraine (France)

Honeycomb

Makes 1 tray of honeycomb

200g (7oz) caster (superfine) sugar

6 tablespoons honey

2 teaspoons bicarbonate of soda (baking soda)

1 teaspoon finely chopped rosemary

- Lightly grease and line a 20 x 20cm baking tray with non-stick baking (parchment) paper.

- Put the sugar and honey in a medium pan over a medium-low heat. Stir with a wooden spoon until the sugar has dissolved – this can take up to 10 minutes, so be patient.

- Once the sugar has dissolved, increase the heat and boil the sugar until you have a golden caramel colour. Remove from the heat, add the bicarbonate of soda (baking soda) then stir until the bubbles start to subside. Stir through the rosemary and carefully tip into the prepared tray. Leave to cool completely.

- Break into shards and serve.

Alternative cheese pairings: Humboldt Fog (USA), Stilton (UK), Délice de Bourgogne (France)

STRONG + MIGHTY CHEESEBOARD

"What's your strongest cheese?" is the question cheesemongers are asked more than any other. People seem to love cheeses that are big, bold and full of intense flavours, and this selection doesn't disappoint.

1. Cornish Kern + Roasted pineapple

There's a burst of tropical flavours when you crunch into a slice of Cornish Kern, a hard crystalline cheese that sits somewhere between Gouda and Comté. A hunk of charred pineapple takes the experience to another level.

2. Stinking Bishop + Pickled cucumber

This pungent cheese from Gloucestershire is well named. Washed in perry, made from a pear variety called Stinking Bishop, it has a powerful aromatic orange rind and bulging texture. The sharp crunch of pickles provides a refreshing contrast.

3. Cashel Blue + Date & walnut flapjack

There are spicier blues out there, but Cashel from Tipperary, Ireland, has an all-encompassing creaminess that hits you in waves. The sweet and sticky flapjack adds to the luxury and acts as a counterpoint to the cheese's lingering salty finish.

4. Corra Linn + Spiced poached quince

Errington Cheese in Lanarkshire uses raw milk from its flock of Lacaune sheep to make Corra Linn, a hard, grainy cheese with savoury, roasted lamb notes. It pairs perfectly with tender slices of fragrant quince. Scotland's answer to Manchego and membrillo.

Roasted pineapple

Makes 1 roasted pineapple

1 pineapple, peeled, cored, sliced and slices chopped into quarters

olive oil, to drizzle

25g (1oz) brown sugar

salt

• Preheat the oven to 180°C (350°F), Gas Mark 4 and line a baking tray with nonstick baking (parchment) paper.

• Spread out the pineapple slices on the lined baking tray. Drizzle the pineapple with olive oil and sprinkle with the sugar and some salt.

• Shake to ensure they are all coated.

• Roast the slices in the oven until golden, about 30 minutes. This will keep for up to 1 week in the refrigerator.

Alternative cheese pairings: Parmigiano Reggiano (Italy), Gouda (Holland), Appenzeller (Switzerland)

Pickled cucumber

Makes 2 pickled cucumbers

FOR THE CUCUMBERS

2 cucumbers or 4 pickling cucumbers (see note)

salt

FOR THE PICKLING LIQUOR

290ml (10½oz) water

145g (5¼ oz) sugar

1 star anise

1 clove

1 cinnamon stick

1 teaspoon black pepper

1 teaspoon coriander seeds

1 teaspoon fennel seeds

580ml (1¼ pints) white wine vinegar

• Slice the cucumbers widthways into 1cm (½-inch) thick slices. Add them to a colander in the sink and dust them with salt, then allow to sit for at least 45 minutes. The salt will draw out the moisture from the cucumbers.

• Meanwhile, combine the pickling liquor ingredients in a pan and bring to the boil. Remove from heat as soon as it comes to the boil and allow to cool.

• Brush off any excess salt from the cucumbers and drain.

• Pack the cucumbers into jars and pour over the pickling liquor. Tightly seal and then leave for at least 4 hours, preferably overnight. Keep them in a cool dark place. Unopened they will keep for 4 weeks.

Variations
You can swap cucumbers for other vegetables, such as cabbage, radishes, carrots or jalapeños. You can also mix and match with the spices, adding chilli, dill, garlic, ginger, bay leaf, etc.

Note: Pickling cucumbers are shorter and fatter than regular cucumbers. Identifiable by their bumpy and spiny exterior, they have thicker skins and hold up better to life in the pickle liquor.

Alternative cheese pairings: St Nectaire (France), St Tola (Ireland), Taleggio (Italy)

Date & walnut flapjack

Makes 1 tray of flapjacks

125g (4½oz) butter, plus a little
extra for greasing the tray

125g (4½oz) brown sugar

100ml (3½fl oz) date syrup

250g (9oz) porridge oats

100g (3½oz) dates, chopped

100g (3½oz) walnuts, chopped

• Preheat the oven to 170°C (340°F), Gas Mark 3½. Line a baking tray with nonstick baking (parchment) paper and grease with butter.

• Heat the butter, sugar and syrup in a saucepan until the butter is fully melted.

• Put the porridge oats, dates and walnuts into a large bowl, pour over the sugar, butter and syrup mixture, and mix well.

• Pour the flapjack mix into the lined tray; you should aim for it to be about 3cm (1¼-inches) thick.

• Bake for 25 minutes or until starting to turn golden but still soft in middle.

• Allow to slightly cool before cutting into small squares to serve. This will keep in an airtight container for 1 week.

Alternative cheese pairings: Cote Hill Blue (UK), Montagnolo Affine (Germany), Caveman Blue (US)

Spiced poached quince

Makes 2 poached quinces

215ml (7½fl oz) water

215ml (7½fl oz) white wine

65g (2¼oz) caster (superfine)
sugar

½ lemon, sliced

2 star anise

1 cinnamon stick

2 quinces, peeled, cored
and quartered

• Add the water, white wine, sugar, sliced lemon, star anise and cinnamon stick to a saucepan and bring to the boil.

• Turn the temperature down to a simmer, add the quince and poach for around 2 hours, until soft.

• Once cooked, leave to fully cool in the cooking liquid. They will keep in the refrigerator for up to 1 week.

Alternative cheese pairings: Manchego (Spain), Ossau-Iraty (France), pecorino (Italy)

CLASSY + CONTINENTAL(ISH) CHEESEBOARD

British cheesemakers have long taken inspiration from their counterparts across the Channel to create Continental-style cheeses. But rather than just making imitations, they are now fusing different influences from France, Italy, Spain and Holland.

1. Truffled Brie + Pickled grapes
Baron Bigod is Suffolk's answer to Brie-de-Meaux. Soft, yielding and packed with flavours of wild mushrooms and brassica, it's a delicious cheese that is taken to another level with a layer of black truffle. Pickled grapes cut through the intensity with pinpoint acidity.

2. St James + Candied peanuts
This square washed rinder looks a little like Taleggio, but is actually made in Cumbria with raw sheep's milk. Produced in the spring and summer only, it changes with the seasons, ranging from springy to silky soft with rounded malty notes. Candied peanuts pick up on an inherent nuttiness in the cheese, and run with it.

3. Perl Las + Fig-cocoa spread
The delicate bitterness of cocoa and the sticky sweetness of figs are an excellent foil for rich, spicy blues, such as Perl Las. Made in Carmarthenshire, Wales, this squidgy blue follows in the footsteps of Continental classics, such as Fourme d'Ambert and Gorgonzola Dolce, with a mellow piquancy.

4. Coolea + Cumin praline
The Dutch have added cumin seeds to Gouda for centuries. The aromatic spice brings fragrance and crunch to the sweet and nutty cheese. A shard of glassy cumin praline does a similar job with Coolea – a Gouda from Cork in Ireland that tastes of brown butter and hazelnuts.

Pickled grapes

Makes approx. 400g (14oz)

85ml (6 tablespoons) water

85ml (6 tablespoons) sherry vinegar

55ml (2fl oz) white wine vinegar

65g (2¼oz) caster (superfine) sugar

½ teaspoon black pepper

400g (14oz) red grapes

3 sprigs of rosemary

salt

· In a saucepan, combine the measured water, both vinegars, sugar, pepper and a pinch of salt. Bring to the boil, stirring occasionally. Remove from the heat and allow to cool for 10 minutes.

· Remove the grapes from their stems and make a small incision in the end of each grape. Place in a pickling jar with the destemmed rosemary, then pour over the cooled liquid to fully cover the grapes. Seal and refrigerate for 2 days before serving to allow to infuse.

Alternative cheese pairings: Valençay (France), Four Fat Foul (US), St Jude (UK)

Candied peanuts

Makes approx. 150g (5½oz)

125g (4½oz) blanched peanuts

15g (½oz) butter, melted

13g (½oz) icing (confectioners') sugar

13g (½oz) honey

½ teaspoon mixed (apple pie) spice

10g (¼oz) granulated brown sugar

· Preheat the oven to 180°C (350°F), Gas Mark 4. Line a baking tray with nonstick baking (parchment) paper.

· In a large bowl, mix the peanuts, butter, icing (confectioners') sugar, honey and mixed (apple pie) spice.

· Spread evenly on the lined baking tray and cook in the oven for about 12 minutes, stirring them halfway through, until the peanuts have a golden coat.

· Allow to cool for 10 minutes before stirring to break them up and shaking the brown sugar over the top.

Alternative cheese pairings: Maida Vale (UK), Willoughby (USA), Idiazabal (Spain)

Fig-cocoa spread

Makes approx. 180g (6½oz)

100g (3½oz) dried figs

8g (¼oz) cocoa powder

80ml (5 tablespoons) full-fat (whole) milk

- Place all the ingredients in a food processor and blend to a smooth paste.

- This will keep in an airtight container in the refrigerator for 5 days.

Alternative cheese pairings: Gouda (Holland), Gruyère (Switzerland), Spenwood (UK)

Cumin praline

Makes 1 tray of praline

100g (3½oz) caster (superfine) sugar

½ teaspoon cumin seeds

* Note – be careful to avoid skin contact with the caramel at all costs!!

- Line a tray with nonstick baking (parchment) paper, and cut a second sheet of baking paper a similar size.

- In a pan over a low heat, melt the sugar until it reaches a golden colour. Don't stir the sugar. To help it melt evenly, give the pan a little shake.

- Remove from the heat and sprinkle in the cumin seeds.

- Quickly pour the mix onto your lined tray. Cover it with the second sheet of baking paper and spread the mixture evenly across the tray with a rolling pin.

- Leave to set at room temperature. Once set, break up into medium-sized shards to serve with your cheese.

Alternative cheese pairings: Roquefort (France), Rogue River Blue (US), Wigmore (UK)

POURING

+   PAIRING

Is red wine always the best match for cheese? Does cheese go with sparkling wine? And how do you pick one wine for an entire cheeseboard?

These are (some of) the questions that occupy the thoughts of serious cheese heads. So we thought we'd join forces with two of London's best wine minds in an attempt to get to the heart of what really makes a killer match.

There was, of course, plenty of cheese and wine on hand to stimulate the discussion.

The cheese and wine gang:

1. Anjali Douglas [AD]
Wine educator at Wine & Spirit
Education Trust (WSET) School, London

2. Eliza Parkes [EP]
Co-owner of Yardarm, wine shop,
bar and deli, Leyton, London

3. Mathew Carver [MC]
Owner of The Cheese Bar

4. Patrick McGuigan [PM]
Cheese writer and educator

PM: Okay, let's get down to business. What makes a good cheese and wine match?

AD: I'm looking for a match that is greater than the sum of its parts. Take a good cheese and pair with the right wine; they will hopefully elevate each other. One plus one equals three.

EP: I love a perfect pairing. But one cheese matched with one wine is very precise. And to be honest, we don't normally have wine and cheese in that way. Usually you have lots of cheeses and one or two wines.

PM: So we're looking for wines that are good cheese all-rounders then?

MC: I normally go for dry white wine, if there are lots of different cheeses on a board. The acidity cuts through the richness of the cheese. There's a general perception that red wine goes with all cheeses, but I don't think that's true. The tannins often don't get on with the creaminess. It's like one plus one equals zero.

PM: Red wine with cheese is a very British thing. The cheeseboard normally comes out at the end of the meal here, and that's when the red wine or port tends to be open. But I often serve a few slices of cheese at the start of a meal as an aperitif, with a glass of something white and refreshing. Riesling and a soft goats' cheese or dry sherry with a few slices of Manchego.

AD: I love the idea that cheese is not something you have at the end of a meal. Can I make a confession? I find port quite challenging. It can have a strong, spirity flavour because of the way it's made, which can be quite overpowering. I think sherry or Madeira are much more harmonious with cheese. And I totally agree that big reds can squash the flavours in cheese.

MC: We have just as many white wines on our menus as reds. Riesling, Sauvignon Blanc, Albariño and Picpoul are really popular because they've got that zingy acidity.

EP: I agree with all of this, but there are plenty of red wines that are not high in tannins and have decent acidity that can work with lots of cheeses. You can even chill them slightly. Pinot Noir and Gamay fit that category and can work with soft, washed-rind and hard cheeses.

MC: Those are exactly the kinds of reds that we sell a lot of in the restaurants. Also wines such as Blaufränkisch from Austria and Sangiovese from Italy, which have good acidity.

AD: I suppose what we're getting into here is that wines at different ends of the spectrum are tougher to match. So heavy, tannic reds and very light delicate whites are quite polarizing when it comes to cheese. But wines that sit in the middle are often good all-rounders.

EP: Sometimes, though, when you get a good cheese match with a big red or a light white, there's more wow factor. Parmesan and Barolo is wonderful because the salty cheese softens the tannins in the wine and you get more of the fruit flavours.

PM: Can we talk about bubbles? I'm a massive fan of sparkling wines with cheese. The fizz and acidity of Champagne or English sparkling is really refreshing, and you often get honey and toasty notes that work with cheese.

AD: I'm with you on that. I'll sometimes open a bottle of sparkling wine at the end of a meal. You don't always want something sweet or very alcoholic at the end of a big meal. A glass of fizz really resets everyone and perks you up so you're ready to go again. What's exciting about this is that there are lots of great sparkling wines being made in the UK now, which work really well with lots of different cheeses.

EP: English wine is definitely on the up. There are so many new vineyards and producers, who are taking English wine in exciting new directions. We're getting wines now that taste English, rather than copying what happens in France.

MC: The exact same thing is happening in cheese. There are young producers who are creating new cheeses that are unique to the UK. There's lots of mileage in pairing British wines with British cheeses.

PM: You often hear "what grows goes together goes together" about cheese and wine, that the wines made in a particular region go with the local cheeses because they've developed side by side over hundreds of years. There's definitely some truth to it: goats' cheeses from the Loire Valley in France are great with Sauvignon Blanc and Chenin Blanc, which grow locally. And I love Comté and Vin Jaune, which both come from the Jura in France.

AD: Nutty wines like Vin Jaune are often a good match for cheese. They seem to just work with fatty, salty foods generally. I love Oloroso sherry and Manchego for the same reason.

EP: Skin-contact wines fit into that. There are lots more orange wines on wine lists these days, and they often have a nuttiness about them that goes with all sorts of cheeses.

I think that starts to bring the idea of texture in wine. Some wines have more viscosity and higher alcohol. They can be waxy and creamy, and they work really well with cheeses. Viognier, and Grüner Veltliner are good examples.

PM: I like the idea of texture in wine. It's a really big part of the experience of eating cheese – whether it's silky, crumbly or crystalline – so I suppose it makes sense in wine, too. A creamy cheese with a creamy wine is a no-brainer.

EP: Another approach is to think about intensity. If it's a quiet wine, full of light and delicate aromas, then you want a milder cheese that will bring out those subtle notes. But a loud wine that is intense and powerful is much happier with a strong aged cheese.

PM: Finding complementary flavours also works. So a meaty, farmyardy washed-rind cheese with a funky orange wine. But then sometimes contrasting flavours also work well, so salty Roquefort with sweet Sauternes.

MC: So I think we're getting somewhere here. But I'd also like to say that people shouldn't get too hung up on rules. Half the fun of it all is just sitting down with friends and trying different cheeses and wines together and seeing where you end up.

Five steps to cheese and wine nirvana

1. Full-bodied, dry white wines and light reds with low tannins are good cheese all-rounders. Think Riesling and Grüner Veltliner (white) or Pinot Noir and Gamay (red).

2. Bubbles are brilliant. Sparkling wines are great with lots of cheeses because they bring refreshing acidity and fizz.

3. Think about complementary textures and intensities. Delicate wines with delicate cheeses, and powerful cheeses with powerful wines. Creamy cheeses with creamy wines.

4. Complement and contrast. Pick a flavour in the cheese and try to find a wine with complementary notes. Or alternatively contrast the flavour with something different in the wine.

5. Keep tasting. There are always matches that don't conform to these rules and just do their own thing. Keep trying different wines with different cheeses: it's half the fun!

St Ella + Sancerre

This pairing brings back memories for Mathew of being in Sancerre, the small hill-top town where every bar serves a whole Crottin de Chavignol goats' cheese and a glass of Sancerre for 5 euros. St Ella is a British crottin full of similar citrussy and spicy notes that work in the same way with a crisp, cold Sauvignon.

Brefu Bach + Champagne

This soft and fluffy sheep's milk cheese made near Snowdonia in Wales has a delicate acidity and buttery flavour, which is mirrored by the creamy, brioche notes of aged Champagne or English sparkling wine. It's like buttered toast in cheese and wine form (with bubbles).

Brie + rosé

One of Anjali's favourite combos. White wines can be overpowered by a ripe Brie de Meaux, while red wines clash with the creaminess. But dry and slightly darker styles of rosé, such as Tavel from the South of France or Clairet from Bordeaux, achieve a nice balance with the cheese. These rosés have more weight, texture and grip compared to the almost water-white Provençal styles, which means they can stand up to the vegetal notes of the rind, while also bringing red fruit flavours to the party.

Cheshire + Chablis

Chablis, made from Chardonnay in Northern Burgundy, is famous for its minerality and racy acidity. Similar things are said of Appleby's Cheshire, which has a flaky texture and bright citrussy notes that veer into salty mineral flavours. Their complementary characters create a wonderful harmony together.

Ossau Iraty
+ Bordeaux blanc

Nutty meets nutty in this pairing, which combines a hard sheep's milk cheese from the French Pyrenees with an oak-aged white wine Sauvignon Blanc and Semillon blend. Both have hints of roasted hazelnuts and almonds that get along famously. The wine also has a rich, honeyed texture, which meets the savoury sweet cheese head on.

Parmigiano Reggiano
+ Barolo

Italy's most popular hard cheese is aged for a year and more until it is salty, savoury and crystalline. It's a magnificent match for the high tannins and acidity of Barolo, the intense, long-lived red made with Nebbiolo grapes in Piedmont. The salt in the cheese softens the tannins, allowing complex floral and leather notes to flourish.

Taleggio + Beaujolais

Washed-rind cheeses are tricky to match because their pungent rinds can easily overpower many wines. Taleggio has a wonderful yeasty flavour and glossy texture, which works surprisingly well with the red fruit flavours of Beaujolais, especially cru wines such as Morgon. The perfumed raspberry notes sit happily side by side with the funky cheese.

Comté + Vin Jaune

The Jura mountains in France are home to Comté, a fruity, caramelly cheese, which pairs beautifully with the local wine Vin Jaune. It's an unusual wine made with local Savagnin grapes, aged under a thin layer of yeast (in a similar way to Fino and Manzanilla sherry). Bone dry with a rich texture, it dovetails with the brown butter and hazelnut notes of the cheese.

Bleu d'Auvergne
+ Coteaux du Layon

Eliza says this match between a creamy French blue and dessert wine from the Loire has got people into sweet wine when they thought it wasn't for them. Something about the saltiness and acidity of the cheese balances perfectly with the sweetness and high acidity in the wine. The joy about Coteaux du Layon is that it's lighter and less sweet than something like a Sauternes, so it is much easier going.

Stilton + Madeira

Port and Stilton is a classic match, but there's another Portuguese fortified wine that works a treat with England's savoury, biscuity blue. Madeira has fresh acidity (especially the Sercial variety) alongside dried fruit and roasted nut notes, which make it a more refreshing partner for Stilton.

BEYOND WINE

Bix + sparkling elderflower

Bix from Oxfordshire is a triple-cream cheese, made by adding double (heavy) cream to cows' milk. The resulting cheese, which has a delicate, wiggly rind, is soft, velvety and coats the mouth, but still has a crème fraîche tang. The bubbles of a sparkling elderflower soft drink break up the cream and add sophisticated notes of flowers and hedgerows.

Golden Cross + green tea

A lovely way to finish a meal. A few slices of this goats' log from Sussex with a cup of well-steeped green tea makes for an intriguing friendship. The damp, earthy notes of the tea seem to bring out a minerally, almost seaweedy note in the cheese. A mellow match.

Chabichou du Poitou + wheat beer

This cylindrical goats' cheese from the Loire Valley has a wrinkly rind, semi-soft texture and a fabulous floral and peppery flavour. The spicy notes and silky texture of wheat beer, especially Belgian "witbiers", marry up with the cheese in a most refreshing way.

Brie + lager

Bries are tricky to match with wine. The gooey paste clashes with reds, while white wines seem to accentuate the bitterness in the rind. But a crisp pilsner is made for the job. The bubbles clean up the goo, while the relatively neutral flavour of the lager allows the Brie to fully express itself.

Camembert de Normandie + sake

There are numerous sake styles, but it's the less polished Junmai style that really seems to hit it off with cheese. The umami flavour and rich texture work with everything from soft goats' cheeses to Gruyère, but it's at its best when taking on the cabbage and wild mushroom notes of a ripe Camembert de Normandie.

Montgomery's Cheddar + cider

An all-time classic combination that never gets old. Cheddar makers and (hard) cider makers live and work cheek by jowl in Somerset, so it's natural that the fruits of their labour are allies. Brothy Montgomery's Cheddar, made in North Cadbury, Somerset, with the toffee apple notes of a local medium–dry cider, such as Burrow Hill, is a pairing for the ages.

Smoked Cheddar + whisky

Even the most powerful red wines can struggle to take on a traditionally smoked Cheddar. But a peaty single malt whisky is a different matter. Put the two together and the smoke clears to reveal fruitiness in both the cheese and the whisky. Top tip: a splash of water in the whisky will open up the flavour.

Epoisses + vermouth

Epoisses from the Burgundy region of France is the archetypal stinky washed-rind cheese. Viscous and whiffy with intense beefy and farmyard flavours, it needs a drink with a similar disposition. Step forward red vermouth – a kind of fortified wine flavoured with botanicals. Popular in Italy, it's sweet, herbal and bitter and has enough intensity to take on the mighty Epoisses.

Gorgonzola Dolce + sloe gin

Lombardy meets the hedgerows of Britain. Lusciously soft Gorgonzola Dolce from Northern Italy often has a boozy and salty quality that makes it a good match for liqueurs. The plummy, herbaceous notes of sloe gin pick up on the fruitiness in the cheese, but also contrast with the salt.

Harbourne Blue + mead

A most unusual blue cheese from Devon, Harbourne is made with goats' milk and is floral and fruity. It's a delicately balanced cheese that needs something equally gentle and refreshing. A light sparkling session mead, made by fermenting honey, is just the ticket.

TOOLS OF THE TRADE

1. Cheese wires or cheese cutters are the workhorse of the cheese counter. The thin wire, which has a handle at one end and is attached to a plastic board at the other, can be pulled through almost any cheese, from soft to hard and small to large. Quick and easy to use and clean, it gives a precise, sharp cut.

2. Large, drum-shaped Parmigiano Reggiano and Grana Padano cheeses are too big and hard to cut using a wire. Instead, specialist "tagliagrana" knives are used to crack them open. First a hooked knife is used to score the thick rind, then strong blades are pushed into the cheese at key points. These are levered so that the cheese cracks in two.

3. Known as "rocker" or Dutch cheese knives, these curved blades are used for cutting very hard cheeses, such as Gouda. The cheesemonger holds both ends and leans on the blade, gently rocking at the same time.

4. Cheese planes are often used by mongers to cut very thin slices from cheeses to give to customers to taste.

5. Cheese irons (known as cheese triers in the US) are used to assess how a whole cheese is maturing, without having to cut it open. The long, sharp tool is pushed into the cheese and turned to cut a plug of cheese. This cross section of cheese is then pulled out and can be assessed for appearance, aroma and texture.

TOOLS OF THE TABLE

1. A large, sharp kitchen knife is perfect for cutting big, hard cheeses, such as Parmesan and Gouda, into more manageable wedges for the board.

2. Knives with holes are designed for soft and gooey cheeses, such as Brie and soft goats' cheeses. The gaps give a clean cut and prevent the blade from dragging through the paste and becoming sticky and clogged up.

3. Full bladed knives are better suited to wedges of hard cheeses, such as Cheddar, Comté and Manchego. The fork on the end is used to spear and share slices with guests.

4. Cheese planes are great for shaving wafer-thin slices from hard and semi-hard cheeses, such as Gruyére and Tommes. The ultra-thin slices melt in your mouth.

5. Small hatchets are fun for cleaving small cheeses, which come in various shapes, from pyramids and cylinders to discs and logs.

HOW TO CUT CHEESE

Life is too short to worry about how to cut cheese. Cheese is there to be enjoyed whichever way you slice it. But there are a few rules of thumb.

The first is that you should aim to slice from the centre to the rind. The heart of a cheese will have different flavours and textures to the area close to the rind, so by cutting a cross section, you get to experience all the differences. If you cut the nose off a wedge of cheese, you are only getting the centre (and robbing everyone else of the pleasure at the same time).

The other tip is to think about cutting cheeses so that everyone gets an equal share of the rind, and nobody is left with a slice that is all rind and no paste.

1. Cheeses in pyramid, cube, ball and tower shapes should be cut vertically into wedges, from top to bottom.

2. Log- and brick-shaped cheeses should be cut into circular or rectangular slices, working your way along the cheese.

3. Small and medium-sized whole cheeses, which are round, square or hexagonal, should be portioned wagon-wheel style into wedges, like cutting a cake.

4. Large wedges of cheese, such as Cheddar, can be placed on their side and cut into long triangles. For wide disc-shaped cheeses, such as Gruyére, wedges can be cut crossways into batons, before slicing lengthways when you are closer to the rind on the side.

HOW TO WRAP CHEESE

1. Place the paper in a portrait position and put the cheese in the centre (with the nose pointing away from you, if wrapping a wedge). Make sure the waxed side of the paper is in contact with the cheese (it's shinier than the unwaxed side).

Waxed paper, which is coated on one side with paraffin or soy bean wax, is ideal for wrapping almost all types of cheese because it prevents moisture loss, while letting the cheese breathe. It's popular with cheesemongers who also often sell it in their shops and online (see page 22 for more on how to store cheese).

This wrapping technique doesn't require any tape and can be used for various cheese shapes, from wedges and towers to logs and rounds.

4. Push the sides of the paper down against the table and fold the edges inwards, close against the cheese, so they meet in the middle to create a triangle on each side. It's just like wrapping a present.

2. Lift up the ends of the paper so they meet in the middle. Fold the edges together to form a 1cm (½-inch) pleat.

3. Continue to fold the pleat downwards until it sits snugly across the middle of the cheese. You want the paper tight against the cheese, but not so tight you squash it.

5. Fold the newly created triangular flaps neatly underneath the cheese.

6. The weight of the cheese keeps the wrapping in place and keeps the paper close against the cheese.

Style	UK	
Fresh	Buffalicious Mozzarella (buffalo)	Pant-Ys-Gawn, Wales (goat)
	Connage Crowdie, Scotland	Perroche (goat)
	Graceburn	Rosary (goat)
	La Latteria Mozzarella, Scamorza & Burrata	Somerset Ricotta
	Laverstoke Mozzarella (buffalo)	Sussex Slipcote (sheep)
Wrinkly rinds (yeast ripened)	Bix	St Ella (goat)
	Brefu Bach, Wales (sheep)	St Jude
	Dorstone (goat)	Sinodun Hill (goat)
	Elrick Log, Scotland (goat)	Sir Lancelot, Scotland (sheep)
	Golden Cross (goat)	Tor (goat)
	Little Lepe (goat)	
	Pavé Cobble (sheep)	
Bloomy rinds (mould ripened)	Ailsa Craig, Scotland (goat)	Paddy's Milestone, Scotland
	Ballylisk Triple Rose, Northern Ireland	Ragstone (goat)
	Baron Bigod	Tunworth
	Clava Connage Brie, Scotland	Waterloo
	Finn	Wigmore (sheep)
	Flower Marie (sheep)	Winslade
Semi-hard	Allerdale (goat)	St Helena
	Anster, Scotland	Stonebeck Wensleydale
	Ashcombe	Thelma's Caerffili, Wales
	Appleby's Cheshire	Ticklemore (goat)
	Cornish Yarg	Witheridge
	Gorwydd Caerphilly	Westray Wife, Scotland
	Kirkham's Lancashire	Yoredale Wensleydale
	Martell Single Gloucester	Yorkshire Pecorino Fresco (sheep)
Hard	Ayrshire Dunlop, Scotland	Spenwood (sheep)
	Berkswell (sheep)	Teifi, Wales
	Bonnet, Scotland (goat)	Wyfe of Bath
	Corra Linn, Scotland (sheep)	Yorkshire Pecorino (sheep)
	Doddington	
	Rachel (goat)	
	Sparkenhoe Red Leicetser	

Note: Cheeses are all made with cows' milk unless stated. UK cheeses are all English unless stated.

Europe		USA	
Burrata, Italy	Ricotta, Italy (sheep)	Bellwether Ricotta, California	Ms. Natural, California (goat)
Feta, Greece (sheep, goat)	Ricotta Salata, Italy	Capriole Fresh Chevre, Indiana (goat)	Seal Cove Goat Milk Feta, Maine (goat)
Halloumi, Cyprus (sheep, goat)	Scamorza, Italy	Caputo Bros. Mozzarella, Pennsylvania	Smokey Mountain Round, North Carolina (goat)
Mascarpone, Italy		Goat Lady Creamy Original, North Carolina (goat)	The Real Philly Schmear, Pennsylvania
Mozzarella di Bufala Campana, Italy (buffalo)		Maplebrook Mozzarella, Vermont	Westfield Capri, Massachusetts (goat)
Crottin de Chavignol, France (goat)	Sainte-Maure de Touraine, France (goat)	Bijou, Vermont (goat)	Tuffet, Missouri (cow, sheep)
Kato, Belgium (goat)	Saint-Félicien, France	Bonne Bouche, Vermont (goat)	Wabash Cannonball, Indiana (goat)
La Tur, Italy (cow, goat, sheep)	Saint-Marcellin, France	Intergalactic, Pennsylvania	
Monte Enebro, Spain (goat)	Selles-sur-Cher, France (goat)	Sofia, Indiana (goat)	
Perail, France (sheep)	St Tola, Ireland (goat)		
Rocamadour, France (goat)	Valençay, France (goat)		
Banon, France (goat)	Cremoso, Spain (sheep)	Dirt Lover, Missouri (sheep)	Moses Sleeper, Vermont
Brie de Meaux, France	Délice de Bourgogne, France	Green Hill, Georgia	Mt. Tam, California (triple cream)
Brie de Melun, France	Robiola, Italy (goat)	Harbison, Vermont	St Stephen, New York (triple cream)
Brillat-Savarin, France		Haystack Peak, Colorado (goat)	Trillium, Indiana (triple cream)
Camembert de Normandie, France		Humboldt Fog, California (goat)	
Chaource, France		Kunik, New York (cow, goat, triple cream)	
Coulommiers, France			
Asiago, Italy	Vacherin Fribourgeois, Switzerland	Appalachian, Virginia	Point Reyes Toma, California
Fontina, Italy		Ashbrook, Vermont	Thomasville Tomme, Georgia
Jarlsberg, Norway		Cloud Cap, Washington	Vella Monterey Jack, California
Morbier, France		Cumberland Tomme, Tennessee	
Provolone, Italy		Pawlet, Vermont	
St Nectaire, France			
Tomme Crayeuse, France			
Tomme de Savoie, France			
Cais na Tire, Ireland (sheep)	Mimolette, France	Anabasque, Wisconsin (sheep)	St. Malachi, Pennsylvania
Cantal, France	Old Groendal, Belgium	Aries, California, (sheep)	Seascape, California (cow, goat)
Coolea, Ireland	Ossau Iraty, France (sheep)	Invierno, Vermont (sheep, cow)	Seven Sisters, Pennsylvania
Garroxa, Spain (goat)	Pecorino Romano, Italy (sheep)	Marieke Gouda, Wisconsin	Vella Dry Jack, California
Gouda, Holland	Pecorino Sardo, Italy (sheep)	Providence, North Carolina (goat)	Verano, Vermont (sheep)
Idiazabal, Spain (sheep)	Salers, France		
Killeen, Ireland (goat)	Tête de Moine, Switzerland		
Manchego, Spain (sheep)			

Style	UK	
Cheddar	Cheddar Gorge	Quicke's
	Hafod, Wales	St Andrews, Scotland
	Isle of Mull, Scotland	Westcombe
	Keen's	Winterdale Shaw
	Montgomery's	
	Pitchfork	
Hard cooked	Cornish Kern	
	Lincolnshire Poacher	
	Old Winchester	
Washed-rind	Admiral Collingwood	Ogleshield
	Baronet	Rollright
	Celtic Promise, Wales	St Cera
	Edmund Tew	St James (sheep)
	Eve (goat)	Stinking Bishop
	Francis	
	Golden Cenarth, Wales	
	Maida Vale	
Blue	Barkham Blue	Mrs Bell's Blue (sheep)
	Beauvale	Perl Las, Wales
	Beenleigh Blue (sheep)	Pevensey Blue
	Biggar Blue, Scotland (goat)	Sparkenhoe Blue
	Blue Clouds	Sparkenhoe Shropshire Blue
	Buffalo Blue (buffalo)	Stichelton
	Cote Hill Blue	Strathdon Blue, Scotland
	Colston Bassett Stilton	Young Buck, Northern Ireland
	Cropwell Bishop Stilton	
	Devon Blue	
	Harbourne Blue (goat)	
	Hebridean Blue, Scotland	
	Kearney Blue, Northern Ireland	
	Lanark Blue, Scotland (sheep)	
	Leeds Blue (sheep)	

Note: Cheeses are all made with cows' milk unless stated. UK cheeses are all English unless stated.

Europe		USA	
Hegarty's, Ireland Coolattin, Ireland		Beecher's Flagship Reserve, Washington Bleu Mont Bandaged Cheddar, Wisconsin Cabot Cloth-bound, Vermont Fiscalini Old World Cheddar, California	Flory's Truckle, Missouri Grafton Cloth-bound, Vermont Imperial Buck, Wisconsin Shelburne Cloth-bound, Vermont The Stag, Wisconsin
Abondance, France Appenzeller, Switzerland Bergkäse, Germany Beaufort, France Comté, France Emmenthal, Switzerland L'Etivaz, Switzerland Gruyère, Switzerland	Grana Padano, Italy Parmigiano Reggiano, Italy Piave, Italy	Alpha Tolman, Vermont Pleasant Ridge Reserve, Wisconsin Roth Kase Grand Cru, Wisconsin San Joaquin Gold, California Tarentaise, Vermont	
Azeitão, Portugal (sheep) Durrus, Ireland Epoisses, France Gubbeen, Ireland Langres, France Limburger, Germany Milleens, Ireland Mont d'Or, France	Munster, France Raclette de Savoie, France Reblochon, France Taleggio, Italy Torta de Barros, Spain (sheep)	Chalet Limburger, Wisconsin Dorset, Vermont Foxglove, Indiana Grayson, Virginia Hooligan, Connecticut Oma, Vermont Reading, Vermont Red Hawk, California (triple cream)	Rush Creek, Wisconsin Widmer's Brick, Wisconsin Willoughby, Vermont Winnemere, Vermont Whitney, Vermont
Basajo, Italy (sheep) Bleu d'Auvergne, France Bleu des Basques, France (ewe) Blu di Bufala, Italy (buffalo) Blu di Capra, Italy (goat) Cabrales, Spain Cashel Blue, Ireland Chiriboga Blue, Germany Crozier Blue, Ireland (sheep) Fourme d'Ambert, France Gorgonzola Dolce and Piccante, Italy Montagnolo Affine, Germany Roquefort, France (sheep) Valdeón Picos Europa, Spain (cow, goat)		Bayley Hazen, Vermont Caveman Blue, Oregon Cayuga Blue, New York (goat) Indigo Bunting, Wisconsin Maytag Blue, Iowa Point Reyes Original Blue, California Rogue River Blue, Oregon Shakerag Blue, Tennessee Smokey Blue, Oregon	

Where to Buy Good Cheese

This is a small selection of great shops to visit, chosen because they also have good online shops. But there are hundreds to explore. We recommend that you to find your local shop and use it!

UK

England:

Brindisa, London
brindisa.com

Buchanans Cheesemonger, London
buchananscheesemonger.com

Funk, London
thecheesebar.com/funk

George & Joseph, Leeds
georgeandjoseph.co.uk

Jericho Cheese Company, Oxford
jerichocheese.co.uk

La Fromagerie, London
lafromagerie.co.uk

Mons Cheesemongers, London
mons-cheese.co.uk

Neal's Yard Dairy, London
nealsyarddairy.co.uk

Paxton & Whitfield, London & Bath
paxtonandwhitfield.co.uk

The Cheese Society, Lincoln
thecheesesociety.co.uk

The Courtyard Dairy, Yorkshire
thecourtyarddairy.co.uk

The Fine Cheese Co, Bath & London
finecheese.co.uk

Scotland:

George Mewes, Edinburgh & Glasgow
georgemewescheese.co.uk

IJ Mellis, Edinburgh, Glasgow & St Andrews
mellischeese.net

Wales:

The Welsh Cheese Company, Cardiff
welshcheesecompany.co.uk

Ty Caws, Cardiff
tycaws.com

Northern Ireland:

Indie Füde, Belfast
indiefude.com

Mike's Fancy Cheese, Belfast
mfcheese.com

Europe

Alte Milch, Berlin
altemilch.de

Affineurs van Tricht, Antwerp
kaasaffineursvantricht.be

Laurent Dubois, Paris
fromageslaurentdubois.fr

Möllans Ost, Malmo
mollansost.com

Quesería Cultivo, Madrid
queseriacultivo.com

Sheridans Cheesemongers, Dublin
sheridanscheesemongers.com

Volpetti, Rome
volpetti.com

USA

Antonelli's Cheese Shop, Austin, Texas
antonellischeese.com

Beautiful Rind, Chicago
beautifulrind.com

Bedford Cheese Shop, New York
bedfordcheesshop.com

DeLaurenti Food & Wine, Seattle
delaurenti.com

Di Bruno Bros, Philadelphia
dibruno.com

Formaggio Kitchen, Boston
formaggiokitchen.com

La Fromagerie, San Francisco
lafromageriesf.com

Murray's Cheese, New York and nationwide
murrayscheese.com

Further Reading

A Cheesemonger's Compendium of British & Irish Cheese, Ned Palmer, 2021

A Cheesemonger's History of the British Isles, Ned Palmer, 2020

American Farmstead Cheese, Paul Kindstedt, 2005

A Portrait of British Cheese, Angus D. Birditt, 2022

Cheese & Culture: A History of Cheese and its Place in Western Civilization, Paul Kindstedt, 2013

Composing the Cheese Plate, Brian Keyser & Leigh Friend, 2016

Cowgirl Creamery Cooks, Sue Conley, 2013

Reinventing the Wheel, Bronwen and Francis Percival, 2017

The Sheridans Guide to Cheese, Kevin and Seamus Sheridan, 2015

The Great British Cheese Book, Patrick Rance, 1988

The Oxford Companion to Cheese, Catherine Donnelly (ed), 2016

The Philosophy of Cheese, Patrick McGuigan, 2020

The World Cheese Book, Juliet Harbutt, 2015

Organisations

American Cheese Society (US)
cheesesociety.org

Guild of Fine Food (UK)
gff.co.uk

Oldways Cheese Coalition (US)
oldwayspt.org/programs/
oldways-cheese-coalition

Slow Food (Worldwide)
slowfood.com

Specialist Cheesemakers Association (UK)
specialistcheesemakers.co.uk

Education, magazines & courses

Academy of Cheese
academyofcheese.org

Certified Cheese Professional
cheesesociety.org/american-cheese-society-certifications/

Cheese Science
cheesescience.org

Culture magazine
culturecheesemag.com

Fine Food Digest
gff.co.uk/fine-food-digest-online

La Fédération des Fromagers de France
fromagersdefrance.com

Microbial Foods
microbialfoods.org

School of Artisan Food
schoolofartisanfood.org

Glossary of Cheesemaking Terms

Acidification
The process of lowering the pH of milk and curd during cheesemaking. This is typically done by adding starter cultures (lactic acid bacteria), which ferment the lactose into lactic acid.

Alpines
Typically large, hard cooked cheeses that are made in the mountains. Gruyère, Comté and Emmenthal are all examples.

Artisan cheese
There is no formal or legal definition of "artisan cheese", but we use the term to describe cheeses made by hand on a small scale in a traditional way, often on a farm.

Breakdown
The soft, often gooey, layer beneath the rind or around blue veins where cultures have changed the texture of the paste. In the US, the breakdown beneath rinds is known as the creamline.

Casein
The name of a family of proteins in milk, which are the building blocks of cheese.

Cheddaring
Cheddaring is the process of stacking and turning blocks of drained curd to further acidify the curds and draw more moisture (whey) out. It's a key part of the Cheddar-making process, but is also used in other cheeses.

Cheese iron (cheese trier)
A sharp, long tool used for taking samples from whole cheeses without having to cut them open. The iron is pushed into the body of the cheese and turned to cut a cross section of the cheese, which is then withdrawn and can be assessed. The plug of cheese is then pushed back into the whole cheese.

Cheese mites
Microscopic insects (*Acarys siro*), which feed on cheese moulds and can compromise the integrity of the rind, leading to cracking and discoloration. They are particularly troublesome on cloth-bound Cheddars. Cheesemakers have various techniques for removing them, from brushing and vacuuming cheeses by hand to using robots to do the job.

Coagulation
The process of curdling milk so that it changes from a liquid into a solid (curd). This can be done in different ways: by using enzymes (rennet), through acidification, or using a combination of acidity and heat.

Cultures
A collective term for bacteria, moulds and yeasts used in cheesemaking.

Curd
The wobbly blancmange-like mass created by coagulating milk (see above), which mainly comprises proteins, fat and water (whey).

Cutting the curd
Part of the cheesemaking process. Cutting the curd into smaller pieces using knives, a ladle or hands removes whey (water) from the curd. The smaller you cut, the more whey is released and you end up with a drier cheese.

Farmhouse cheese
A cheese made on a farm with milk from the farm.

Fresh cheese
A young cheese that has no rind, such as goats' curd, mozzarella or mascarpone.

Geotrichum candidum
A yeast that creates a wrinkly rind on cheeses and breaks down the paste underneath. Common on goats' cheeses, such as Crottin de Chavignol and Sinodun Hill.

Hard cooked cheeses
Cheeses that are made by scalding (heating) the curds after cutting to high temperatures (over 50°C/120°F) to drive more moisture from the curd and create a drier final cheese. Alpine cheeses and Parmigiano Reggiano are good examples.

Lactic cheese
Cheeses that are made predominantly by coagulating the milk through acidification (see above) caused by starter cultures converting lactose into lactic acid. Soft, tangy goats' cheeses are often made this way.

Lactose

The natural sugar in milk.

Lactose intolerance

Different to an allergy, lactose intolerance is the inability to digest milk sugars. There is virtually no lactose in many hard aged cheeses and low levels in many mould-ripened and blue cheeses because it is converted into lactic acid during the cheesemaking process. Lactose levels also decline the longer a cheese is matured. Fresh cheeses, such as cream cheese, mozzarella, feta and ricotta, and processed cheese where dairy products are blended with cheese, do however contain lactose.

Mould-ripened cheese

Cheeses that have moulds and yeasts growing on the rind that break down the paste underneath, making the texture softer and creating different flavours.

Pasteurization

The process of heat treating milk to deactivate potential pathogens. This can be done in two ways. High Temperature Short Time or "flash" pasteurization: 72°C (161°F) for 15 seconds. Low Temperature Long Time or "batch" pasteurization: 63°C (145°F) for 30 minutes.

Penicillium candidum (AKA Penicillium camemberti)

The bloomy white mould found on mould-ripened cheeses, such as Brie and Camembert.

Penicillium roqueforti

The blue mould used to make blue cheeses.

Piercing

The process of piercing blue cheeses with needles during maturation to allow oxygen to enter and activate the blue moulds inside the cheese.

Raw milk

Milk that has not been heated above 40°C (104°F) prior to cheesemaking.

Rennet

An enzyme produced in the stomachs of young animals (calves, kids, lambs), or extracted from plants or other vegetarian sources. It is added to milk to make it coagulate (see opposite).

Salt

Added to all cheeses as a preservative and to enhance flavour.

Skimming

Taking some or all of the fat (cream) out of milk. This used to be done by literally skimming the cream from the milk, but is now more typically done with a centrifuge. The cream can be used to make butter or cream.

Starter cultures

"Good" lactic acid bacteria that are added to milk to start acidification. The bacteria convert the lactose into lactic acid. Starter cultures play a part in coagulation, food safety and flavour in the final cheese.

Territorial cheeses

British cheeses named after the area or county in which they were originally made, e.g. Wensleydale.

Thermization

There is no legal definition for thermized milk, but it involves the heat treatment of milk to around 57–63°C (135–145°F) for 15 seconds to reduce pathogens and spoilage bacteria. Cheeses made with thermized milk are technically unpasteurized, but are not seen as true "raw milk" cheeses by many European cheesemakers. However, the US Food and Drug Administration classifies thermized cheeses as "raw milk" because they have not been fully pasteurized.

Washed-rind cheeses

Cheeses whose rinds are smeared, or "washed", with brine or a mix of brine and alcohol to encourage pungent bacteria and yeasts to grow. The rinds are often orange in colour and can have strong aromas. Epoisses, Stinking Bishop and Taleggio are classic examples.

Whey

The liquid in curd, much of which is drained away during cheesemaking.

Index

Recipe Index

Thank you

Wrangling so many cheeses, recipes and words into book form took more work than either of us ever quite imagined! We couldn't have done it without an excellent crew of cheese heads.

Thank you to Tayler Carver, who put a huge amount of work into these pages, from testing recipes to telling tales of the grilled cheese frontline.

Also a big shout out to Lizzie Mayson, Rosie Reynolds, Louie Waller, Christy Spring and Sophie Bronze, who worked magic with melted cheese on the photo shoot, and to Michael Curia and David Tanguy from Praline, who brought everything together in such beautiful designs. And thank you to Judith Hannam and Isabel Jessop at Kyle Books for giving us the opportunity to put our cheese lives on the page in the first place!

Thanks also to Jazz Reeves, Estelle Reynolds, Mike Thomson, Eliza Parkes and Anjali Douglas for sharing their cheese and wine knowledge in the book. And to cheesemongers Ealga Shannon for her expert wrapping skills and Nick Bayne for help with the US cheeses.

Chef appreciation
This book celebrates great recipes from The Cheese Bar but it's also a celebration of the many incredible chefs we've had through our doors.

Thank you to Alex Lambert, David Kiss, Jason Seddon, Dominique Goltinger, Graham Firminger, Ross Keeling, Peter Szabo, Fulvio Rupena, Reagan Ellenbroek, Sara Lewis, Kieran Byrne and every other chef who's graced our stoves.

Aside from the chefs, thank you to everyone who has played a part in making The Cheese Bar what it is today. Without the many wonderful and talented people who've made this business their home for months or years we'd never be where we are now. You all rock.

Patrick would like to thank...
A special mention for John Farrand at the Guild of Fine Food, who got me into the cheese life in the first place and has been a supporter and friend ever since. And also big hugs to Tracey Colley at the Academy of Cheese, who has been my partner in crime on many cheese escapades and never fails to crack me up.

Thanks also to all the editors who keep asking me to write about cheese, particularly Michael Lane at Fine Food Digest. And the mongers and makers who have been so kind and helpful down the years. Cheese people are the best people.

Big love to Tony Ennis and Mollie McGuigan for their invaluable feedback and advice.

Most of all, I'd like to say thank you to Ruth, Archie and Bill for putting up with a husband and father who spends far too much time in the cheese shed. All my love, forever.

Mathew would like to thank...
James Stephenson; without him The Cheese Truck would probably not have existed. He's provided endless support, guidance, laughs and tows. Thanks J!

Tayler (again) for her patience, understanding and for keeping me together through the trials and tribulations; we always have a laugh. Suzy and Lauren for the countless hero shifts and for backing me from day one.

Helen Amos for being an absolute rock through the Covid years; Leif Halverson; Pierre Braun, Irvin Miriel and Joey T for the years of trucking, Alex Lambert (again) for his creativity and perseverance in the early days, Ryen for keeping things together while I worked on the book and Hetty for her creative advice.

Finally, respect to the RAC for not cancelling our breakdown cover despite the absurd number of times we called them to the roadside for a 1970s ice-cream van...